THE ART OF JEWELRY

Polymer Clay

TECHNIQUES

PROJECTS

INSPIRATION

KATHERINE DUNCAN AIMONE

LARK CRAFTS

Asheville

Art Director: Dana Irwin

Cover Designer: Barbara Zaretsky

Associate Art Director: Shannon Yokeley

Assistant Art Director: Lance Wille

Art Production Assistant: Jeff Hamilton

Art Intern: Ardyce E. Alspach

Photographer: John Widman

Assistant Editor: Rebecca Guthrie

Editorial Assistance: Delores Gosnell

Editorial Interns: David Squires and
Sue Stigleman

OCLC 11/7/05

Cover:
Sandra McCaw
Snow Flower Brooch, 2005
2 inches (5.1 cm) diameter
Polymer clay, sterling silver bead
PHOTO © ROBERT DIAMANTE

LARK CRAFTS

An Imprint of Sterling Publishing
387 Park Avenue South
New York, NY 10016

If you have questions or comments about
this book, please visit: larkcrafts.com

The Library of Congress has cataloged the hardcover edition as follows:

The art of jewelry : polymer clay: techniques, projects, inspiration /
Katherine Duncan-Aimone.
 p. cm.
 Includes index.
 ISBN 1-57990-616-8 (hardcover)
1. Polymer clay craft. 2. Jewelry making. I. Title.
TT297.D86 2006
745.594'2--dc22

2005035302

10 9 8 7 6 5 4 3

Published by Lark Crafts, An Imprint of Sterling Publishing Co., Inc.
387 Park Avenue South, New York, NY 10016

First Paperback Edition 2011
Text © 2006, Lark Crafts, an Imprint of Sterling Publishing Co., Inc.
Photography © 2006, Lark Crafts, an Imprint of Sterling Publishing Co.;
unless otherwise specified
Illustrations © 2006, Lark Crafts, an Imprint of Sterling Publishing Co.; unless otherwise specified

Distributed in Canada by Sterling Publishing,
c/o Canadian Manda Group, 165 Dufferin Street
Toronto, Ontario, Canada M6K 3H6

Distributed in the United Kingdom by GMC Distribution Services,
Castle Place, 166 High Street, Lewes, East Sussex, England BN7 1XU

Distributed in Australia by Capricorn Link (Australia) Pty Ltd.,
P.O. Box 704, Windsor, NSW 2756 Australia

Manufactured in China

All rights reserved

ISBN 13: 978-1-57990-616-0 (hardcover) 978-1-60059-605-6 (paperback)

For information about custom editions, special sales, and premium and corporate
purchases, please contact Sterling Special Sales Department at 800-805-5489 or
specialsales@sterlingpub.com.

Requests for information about desk and examination copies available to college and
university professors must be submitted to academic@larkbooks.com. Our complete policy
can be found at www.larkcrafts.com.

Many thanks to the creative artists who made this book possible…you who inspire and encourage us to discover our own inventive potential. Your genuine love and enthusiasm for your chosen medium is eloquently referenced in your work.

KDA

contents

The Projects 23

Polymer Clay Jewelry
Introduction

Innovation and creativity have elevated polymer clay to an art form, and new artists are constantly pushing the envelope of this exciting medium. This book showcases the results of that evolution in the form of an impressive collection of sophisticated jewelry by outstanding artists in the field.

The book's 33 projects, created by some of the premier teachers and innovators in contemporary polymer clay, serve to build a repertoire of skills. Each project features several interesting in-process steps, making it simple for you to see the work in stages.

Many techniques are combined, encouraging you to think outside of the box and use the projects as a creative springboard for your own unique pieces. A wide range of forms are included— beads, brooches, pendants, pins, bracelets, and earrings. You'll explore new surface design techniques including texturing, layering, varied finishes, color blending, molding, image transfer, mica shift, and more.

Because of its adaptability and versatility, polymer clay is a natural for jewelry. Jacqueline Lee, a featured artist, notes: "With one medium, you can be a metal-smith, lampworker, illustrator, geologist, tanner, and sculptor." The vast possibilities of this material are tantalizing to artists with backgrounds in a variety of other media—whether ceramics, graphic arts, printmaking, or other creative fields.

Left: Pendants by Lindly Haunani
Top, page 7: Pin by Pier & Penina
Bottom, page 7: Bracelet by SL Savarick

Learn directly from Judith Skinner, well-known teacher and the inventor of the famous "Skinner Blend." Think about color and design by studying the work of Lindly Haunani. Allow Jeffrey Lloyd Dever to guide you through the intricate construction of his beautiful dimensional forms. Learn to think about polymer clay in a different way through the work of cutting edge artists such as SL Savarick, Louise Fischer Cozzi, Alexis Pier, and Penina Meisels.

Through Judith Converse Sober, discover how to combine soldering and polymer clay to make unconventional and exciting pieces. If you prefer to work in a more freeform fashion, Leslie Blackford can help you uncover your sculptural instincts, while Wendy Wallin Mallinow can open your eyes to the eccentric possibilities of the medium. Jennifer Bezingue divulges the mysteries of her glasslike beads, while Mari O'Dell teaches you how to create unique ceramic-like finishes. Stephanie Rubiano shows you the technique of photo transfer on polymer clay, combining it with assemblage. Finally, Sandra McCaw's delicate canework made into a breathtaking objet d'art will convince you once and for all that this medium is unlike any other.

A gallery of sparkling designs by leading artists in the field provides you with more inspiring food for thought as you experiment, learn, and grow through your work. I hope you'll experience the joy of discovery and invention that has served as an energizing force for this group of artists who have so generously shared their work.

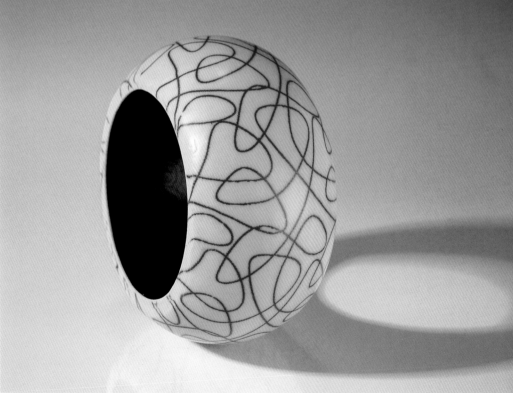

Polymer Clay Jewelry
Basics

By Mari O'Dell

Polymer clay is an amazingly adaptable and versatile material. It can be cut, shaped, sculpted, and made to resemble ivory, bone, stone, wood, ceramic, metal, glass, or other materials. Making jewelry out of this malleable material is a natural choice.

Polymer clay comes in a myriad of colors, ranging from opaque to very transparent. It is also available in pearlescent, fluorescent, metallic, and glittery varieties. It can be tinted, painted, printed, stamped, stenciled, leafed, and molded. Inclusions such as embossing powders, dried herbs, or colored sand can be added to it. After polymer clay is cured or hardened, it can be drilled, carved, painted, punched, cut with decorative-edge scissors, or sanded and buffed.

POLYMER CLAY

Polyvinyl chloride (PVC), or the material used to make white plumbing pipe, is the basic ingredient in polymer clay. The other ingredients are dyes or pigments for color, fillers for bulk, and a plasticizer that allows the clay to be manipulated at room temperature and hardened when properly heated.

There are lots of brands of solid clay from which to choose. You might want to do some research about various brands before buying clay for finer pieces. Eventually, you'll find one you prefer. Each brand has different characteristics, but they're similar enough to be intermixed to create different colors or add strength or flexibility to the form.

Liquid polymer clay, a relatively new product used to create various effects, also comes in opaque, translucent, pearlescent, metallic, or tinted versions. Polymer clay products are available in retail stores and from polymer-based online businesses.

Liquid polymer clay, mixing tray, tinted liquid polymer, and soft brush

Conditioning and Storing

Polymer clay is stiff when cold or if it's been sitting on a shelf, so it's necessary to move the plasticizer to evenly distribute it, making the clay softer and more pliable. For this reason, you'll condition the clay by working it by hand or with a pasta machine.

To condition it by hand, remove the packaging and use a polymer clay tissue blade to slice the block into several ½-inch pieces (photo 1). Place one piece at a time onto a non-porous work surface and roll it before slightly flattening it with an acrylic roller (photo 2). Form the sheet into a log and roll it out to thin it. Fold this piece in half and twist it before rolling it into a ball. Repeat this process several times until the clay is soft and pliable.

To condition polymer clay using a pasta machine, remove the clay from its packaging and slice it into ½-inch pieces before flattening it slightly with an acrylic roller. Prepare the remaining slices in the same manner. Adjust the

Blocks of colorful clay

pasta machine to its widest or thickest setting and roll each slice through the machine (photo 3). Place two sheets of clay together and pass them through the roller again (photo 4). Continue until you have one large sheet of clay. Fold it in half and place the fold into the pasta rollers. Continue doing this about 20 to 25 times until the clay is soft and elastic.

Because polymer clay is heat sensitive, it should be stored in a cool, dry place. Don't leave it in your car or in direct sun. Keep opened packages or works in progress covered in plastic wrap or in plastic storage bags.

Curing

Each brand of polymer clay suggests curing/baking temperatures on its packaging, ranging from 265°F to 275°F. Some translucent clays brown at the higher ranges, so always do a test curing before you begin a good piece.

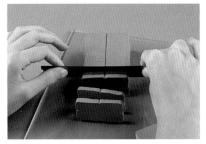

Photo 1

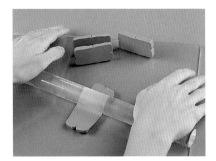

Photo 2

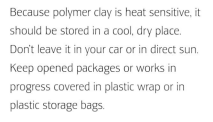

Photo 3

Photo 4

Oven thermometer and surfaces for curing clay: card stock, ceramic tile, polyester quilt batting

Colored chalks, alcohol-based stamp inks, heat-set inks in pads, alcohol-based markers, assorted gel pens, metallic markers, and heat-set metallic ink in pads (see descriptions on pages 12 and 13)

You'll notice that the projects in this book suggest a time and temperature, but you should still read the temperature requirements for any product you are using. Polymer clay formulations often change, and manufacturers alter package instructions to reflect new formulas.

Most ovens cycle up before reaching the temperature set on the dial, so preheat the oven before putting your polymer clay work in for curing. Since ovens vary, you should also calibrate your oven by using a separate interior oven thermometer. Keep an eye on it to see when it has reached the proper temperature

and time. Clay thickness affects the amount of time needed to cure it, and a minimum of 20 minutes is required to properly cure even the thinnest sheet. Always cure clay in a well-ventilated area. Turn on the oven hood, open your windows, and avoid breathing the fumes.

Since the clay gets somewhat soft during the curing period, support thin areas or strands of clay with curls of paper, a bed of polyester quilt batting, or fiberfill on a baking sheet or dish. To prevent glossy spots, cure pieces on paper or cardboard. Make sure that nothing touches the oven elements. Cure beads and other

dimensional pieces on a bead rack or a bed of polyester fiberfill.

TIP: To avoid oven cleanup, you can create a "saggar" or an oven within an oven for curing your clay. It's very simple—you can just make one from two disposable turkey-roasting pans and four spring-loaded clothespins. Place the clay pieces in the bottom pan on a curing tile, cardboard, or polyester fiberfill. Invert the second pan to form a lid and clip it together with clothespins. Add five minutes to your curing time. Clean it by wiping it out with a paper towel.

MATERIALS AND SUPPLIES

The following art and craft materials are compatible with polymer clay and can be mixed or applied to it to create various effects. Many are used as inclusions in the clay, while others are added to the surface. Other materials listed are used for stock functions.

■ *Embossing powders:* Embossing powders are especially effective when used with translucent clay. Mix them into the clay by sprinkling them on a sheet of clay (photo 5). Fold the clay into a packet and seal the edges (photo 6). Carefully run it through the pasta machine until the clay and powders are combined (photo 7). Clear embossing powder can also be applied to flat clay surfaces and heated to form a glaze (photo 8).

Photo 5

Photo 6

Photo 7

Photo 8

■ *Glitter:* Glitters made for rubber-stamping tend to work well as inclusions in polymer clay. Test the heat resistance of any glitter you plan to use for a major project at the temperature you'll be using to cure the clay. Add glitter to clay using the same method as embossing powders.

■ *Mica powders:* These powders add iridescent color to your work (photo 9). They can be mixed with opaque or translucent liquid polymer. If used in powder form, polymer clay must be sealed with a surface varnish to prevent rub-off.

Photo 9

■ *Metal leaf and tooling foils:* Both composition and real metal leaf work well with polymer clay. When working with metal leaf, bring the clay to the book of leaf (photo 10), and use the separator sheets to help tear it off (photo 11). To protect them after they're applied, seal them with a surface varnish or cover them with a sheet of transparent clay.

Photo 10

Photo 11

■ *Other inclusions:* Partially baked clay can be grated and added to clay for color and unusual textures. Other inclusions such as dried herbs and colored sand are also used in polymer clay to change the texture.

■ *Acrylic paints:* These paints adhere to polymer clay and don't fade during curing. You can use them to paint, stamp, or silkscreen on the surface of the clay. You can also use certain colors to create an antique look.

Pearlized paints, acrylic paints, pearl powders, embossing powders, metallic rub ons, brushes, fine glitters, metal leaf, and colored foils

■ *Heat-set and alcohol-based rubberstamp inks:* These inks can be stamped on the clay's surface by inking a stamp (photo 12) and transferring the image to clay (photo 13). To add color to liquid clay, mix bottled inks with them (photo 14). Use them to create a glazed look on textured clay (photo 15). When you use liquid polymers tinted with alcohol-based inks, they speed up the drying time of the liquid polymer. You can also use liquid polymers tinted with inks to create raised designs. Use a squeeze bottle with a fine metal tip to trail the designs on a bead surface or polymer base (photo 16). Cure the raised designs with a heat gun. Add as many details as you wish and cure again (photo 17). When you're done, cure the piece at 275°F for 20 minutes.

Photo 13

Photo 15

Photo 12

Photo 14

Photo 16

Photo 17

■ *Artist's pastels and chalks:* When mixed with clay, or brushed on, these products add color and texture. They should be sealed with a surface varnish to prevent them from rubbing off.

■ *Alcohol-based markers:* These can be used on raw or cured clay for drawing, lettering, or coloring. They become permanent after curing or can be covered by an ultra-thin sheet of translucent clay or a surface varnish.

■ *Water-slide and transfer decal papers:* These papers can be used to transfer images onto polymer clay surfaces and should be sealed with varnish, translucent liquid polymer, or clear embossing powder.

■ *Mold-making material:* Two-part silicone mold-making compound is wonderful for creating crisp, flexible molds used to create multiples (see page 16).

■ *Adhesives:* To attach polymer clay to glass, paper, cardboard, or metal, roughen the surface of the substrate, then apply a PVA-based white craft glue in a thin coat and let it dry completely. Apply the polymer clay, and when you cure the piece, it will bond to its support. Cyanoacrylate glue is used to bond cured clay to metal (such as findings), glass, and other pieces of cured clay. Don't bake or cure this glue since it might fail at high temperatures.

Louise Fischer Cozzi
Channel Bracelet, 2003
2 ⅝ x ¾ inches (6.7 x 1.9 cm)
Polymer clay, brass; etched, painted, penciled
PHOTO © GEORGE POST

Dayle Doroshow
Golden Plumb Bob Pendant, 2004
4 inches (10.2 cm)
Gold leaf, red brass; transfer
PHOTO © DON FELTON

Sandra McCaw
Leaf Cluster Earrings, 2005
2 ¾ inches long (7 cm)
Translucent polymer clay, gold leaf
PHOTO © ROBERT DIAMANTE

Pasta machine with motor attachment, clay shapers, needle tools, hand drills, acrylic work surface, acrylic rollers, metal knitting needles, slicing blades (flexible and stiff), and tissue blade

BASIC TOOLS AND EQUIPMENT

Your own hands are the best tools imaginable, but the following items will facilitate your work with polymer clay. To begin working with clay, you'll need a work surface, some blades to cut the clay, and a pasta machine for conditioning it. Beyond that, there are many helpful tools that you can add to your collection.

■ *Work surface:* Work with the clay on a smooth, nonporous surface such as acrylic sheeting, tempered glass, tile, marble, or a self-healing cutting mat.

■ *Cutting blades:* To cut clay, you'll need tissue blades made for polymer clay and a craft knife blade (#11) and handle. The tissue blades come in stiff and flexible versions. A stiff one is great for cutting chunks of clay into slices to condition it. A flexible blade works well for cutting out curved shapes. The craft knife will allow you to cut out small details from the clay.

■ *Acrylic rollers:* Small acrylic rollers (or brayers) are used for smoothing the clay and delicate joints, while larger rollers are helpful when you're conditioning clay, smoothing large slabs, and reducing canes.

■ *Pasta machine and motor:* This kitchen tool simplifies clay conditioning and mixing, creating even sheets or layers of clay. Once you've used this machine with polymer, never use it for food preparation again. You can add a motor to the machine, and it will do the cranking for you. This works well if you're using a technique requiring two hands. It also helps when rolling ultra-thin sheets of clay.

■ *Smoothing tools:* Tools are made specifically for smoothing polymer clay, but you can also adapt others such as dental tools. Use a knitting needle to smooth the clay in areas too small for your fingers to reach, or where an extra-light touch is required.

■ *Piercing and drilling tools:* Metal knitting needles and needle tools work well for piercing beads before curing them. Pin vises and bits are also favorite tools of clay artists, used for drilling holes in the clay after curing.

■ *Latex gloves:* Wearing gloves will allow you to roll smooth beads and clay surfaces that are free of fingerprints.

Assorted rubber stamps, cornstarch pounce, texture wheels, and assorted texture plates

Special Tools

Because of the constantly growing interest in polymer clay, new tools are always being developed or adapted. The following descriptions give you an overview of some of the more popular ones.

■ *Texture plates:* A variety of flexible, red rubber texture plates are available on the market and can be used for pressing designs in polymer clay. Some artists have their own designs made into plates. Thin plastic texture sheets can be rolled directly through the pasta machine with your clay to add texture to the surface. Always use a resist of some sort to prevent the plate from sticking to the clay. You can spray on a fine mist of water before pressing it. If you're doing this by hand, always press the center of the plate first and work your way out (photo 1). The clay will release, producing a deeply molded impression (photo 2). Cornstarch bundled in a piece of cotton fabric to form a "pounce" is also a good choice. Tap the powder on the clay's surface and proceed. Other resists include metallic powders, chalks, or metal leaf. Apply metal leaf to clay (photo 3) and press it into a deeply etched stamp to create a surface design (photo 4).

Photo 1

Photo 3

Photo 2

Photo 4

Pier & Penina
Wrapped Texture Cuff, 2005
1½ x 13 x ⅛ inches
(3.8 x 33 x 0.3 cm)
Polymer clay; layered, textured, hand-wrapped

Wendy Wallin Malinow
Woodland Camp, 2005
23⅝ x 1³⁄₁₆ inches (60 x 3 cm)
Polymer clay, Peruvian opal, sterling silver;
hand-fabricated, transfer, carving

■ *Texture wheels:* These tools were designed for tooling thin metal sheets, but have been adapted for use on polymer clay. They can be found at rubberstamp stores. Use them to create lovely patterns on polymer clay. Ink them by rolling them over pads containing heat-set ink before applying them to the clay (photo 5). The surface can be tapped with ink, metallic powders, or chalk after it's textured with the wheels (photo 6).

■ *Molds:* You can make your own mold when you want to replicate one of your designs. Simply impress a block of scrap clay and cure it to make a simple mold. However, there are advantages to using a two-part silicone rubber mold-making material. It requires no curing and will produce a wonderfully crisp and flexible mold that makes it easier to remove the molded piece. If you plan to mold a polymer element in silicone, cure the piece first for easier handling. You can also use found objects as originals to create designs that can be trimmed (photos 7 and 8). To make the molding compound, mix equal parts of the silicone materials

(photo 9) and blend until they form a uniform color (photo 10). Ease the compound over the original, and allow it to sit for about 15 to 20 minutes (or the amount of time suggested by the manufacturer). Flex the mold to remove the original (photo 11). Before you press clay into the silicone mold, spray it with water or tap on cornstarch as a resist.

Photo 7

Photo 8

Photo 5

Photo 9

Photo 6

Photo 10

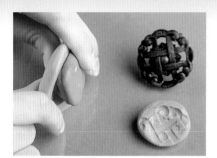

Photo 11

■ *Extruders:* Polymer clay extruders make it possible to produce uniform shapes for caning components and beads, as well as lovely edges and bezels for jewelry (photo 12). Many are available on the market, and some work better than others, so find one that you like. Before you extrude, make sure your clay is very well conditioned. Form a log that's slightly thinner than the diameter of the barrel of the extruder and place it inside (photo 13). Attach the die disc (photo 14) and screw on the cap (photo 15). Press the plunger or squeeze the handle to extrude the clay (photo 16). Trim the extrusion with a tissue blade.

Photo 12

Photo 13

Photo 14

Photo 15

Photo 16

■ *Bead rollers:* These come in several shapes and sizes and allow you to form beads of a uniform size. Roll out a sheet of clay on the widest setting of your pasta machine. Determine the amount of clay needed for your bead and cut away a portion from the sheet (photo 17). Roll the clay between your palms to form a smooth, wrinkle-free ball (photo 18). Place the ball into the bottom of the channel of the roller and replace the top (photo 19). Roll the top back and forth to create a smooth bead shape (photo 20). Cure the bead on a bead rack or a bed of polyester batting.

Photo 17

Photo 18

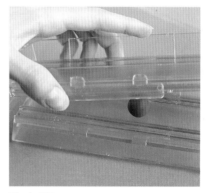

Photo 19

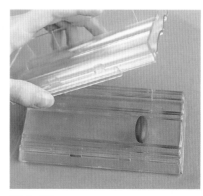

Photo 20

Cane slicer: You can cut cane slices by hand with a tissue blade, but if you want to cut very uniform slices, this piece of equipment is great to own. All variations of this tool have a stage on which the cane is placed, a measuring system with adjustments, and a method of holding the blade rigid and uniform while you cut the clay.

Heat gun: This tool was designed by the rubberstamping industry for use with embossing powders. It's a wonderful tool for quickly curing small bits of clay without having to put them in the oven. A heat gun can also be used to set raised images made in liquid polymer before the final curing.

Cutters and punches: Ceramic punches can be used to cut out shapes from clay (photo 21), and craft punches made for paper can be used on thin sheets of cured clay to cut out detailed shapes (photo 22). You can also use small cookie cutters.

Cane slicer and heat gun

Ripple blades: Made to cut vegetables into rippled slices, these inexpensive blades can be used with clay, allowing you to cut shaped pieces from flat sheets of clay, as well as interesting patterned cuts from stacks or loaves of clay.

Photo 21

Photo 22

Photo 23

Canape cutters, craft punches, cookie cutters, small clay cutters with plunger handles, and ripple cutter blades

Liquid surface treatments, bead reamers, buffing wheel with unsewn muslin wheel, assorted sandpapers, sanding sticks, and sanding sponge blocks

FINISHING AND SURFACE TREATMENTS

Various brands of polymer clay result in slightly different surfaces when cured. These surfaces can be changed or enhanced, depending on the finishing techniques you choose.

Drilling and Carving

After curing, polymer clay elements can be drilled or carved for backfilling, for stringing or hanging, or to make a place to attach a finding. When drilling, mark the placement of the hole. It's a good idea to begin with a drill bit smaller than the final hole before working up to the actual size. Make sure your carving tools are sharp and your work is supported as you carve.

Sanding

Sand the surface of cured polymer clay to create a smooth, glasslike finish. You can sand the piece dry or wet. If you sand the piece without wetting it, make sure to wear a dust mask to protect yourself. Sanding the piece wet eliminates the dust factor. If you're using wet-dry sandpaper or sanding blocks (photo 23), begin with the coarsest grade (400 grit) and sand the piece in water, using a circular motion. Change the water each time you change sandpaper grits, working up to finer grits (600, 800, 1200, or even 1500). The higher grits can be found in automotive supply stores. Dry the clay off and buff it on a soft cotton cloth.

Buffing

To create a highly polished surface, a sanded piece can be buffed on a variable speed buffing wheel fitted with an unsewn muslin buffing head. Before you begin, always remove loose clothing or jewelry that might get caught in the machine. Tie back long hair and wear safety glasses. Hold the piece with both hands and buff it on the lower part of the wheel (photo 24). Keep the piece moving to avoid friction damage.

Photo 24

Liquid and Powder Surfacing Products

To seal and create a shiny surface without sanding and buffing, several commercial products work well. The major polymer manufacturers produce surface varnishes, but you can produce beautiful surfaces by painting or dipping pieces in a liquid acrylic floor finish or acrylic floor wax. These liquids must be allowed to dry in a dust-free environment for at least 24 hours. You can also use these liquid products to seal metal leaf and decal materials that have been cured with polymer clay.

When dealing with flat surfaces, clear embossing rubberstamping powders can be used to finish the surface of polymer clay. Sprinkle on the powders and brush away the excess. Carefully place the piece in a preheated 265°F oven and heat it until the powder is clear and liquid. This product is liquid until cool, so be careful to remove the piece from the oven without tipping it. It will harden as it cools.

Soft glass and Buna cording, various adhesives, clear embossing powders, head pins, eye pins, pin backs, bead caps, tension closures, and crimp beads

Photo 25

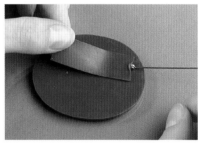

Photo 26

Photo 27

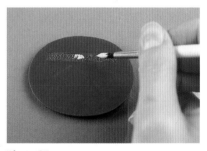

Photo 28

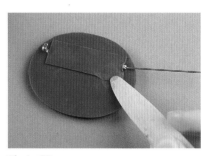

Photo 29

Findings

If you work with jewelry, you're familiar with different types of findings such as eye pins, head pins, pin backs, bails, and clasps. This section explores a couple of basic techniques used by many artists to attach findings to polymer clay jewelry.

ATTACHING A PIN BACK WITHOUT ADHESIVES

You can neatly attach a pin back with a bit of clay instead of adhesive. You may choose to do this in the raw or cured state, depending on your design. Begin by marking the placement of the pin. Use a pin tool to roughen the surface of the clay in this area (photo 25). Sand the metal pin back (photo 26), wipe it with alcohol to remove grease, and allow it to

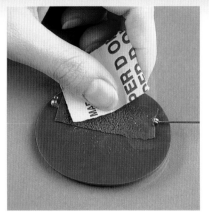

Photo 30

dry. Put a small amount of liquid polymer on the roughened area (photo 27) and place the sanded pin back in position. Roll out a small, thin sheet of clay and trim a small piece to fit over and within the pin back (photo 28). Press the clay in place and smooth it (photo 29). If you wish, press a piece of coarse sandpaper on the polymer sheet to lend it texture (photo 30). Cure in preheated 265°F oven for 20 minutes.

TENSION CLOSURES AND SOFT GLASS CORDING

Most polymer artists are familiar with Buna cord—a solid rubber cord that is popular to use as cording for jewelry. Soft glass cording is a hollow version of rubber cording, making it ideal for adding simple tension closures. To add a closure, trim the cord, select a closure, and place a tiny amount of cynoacrylate glue on one end of the closure (photo 31). Insert this end of the closure into one side of the cord and hold in place for a minute. Slide the other end of the closure into the open end of the cord to secure it.

Photo 31

Stephanie Jones Rubiano
Soda, 2005
3 x 2¼ x ⅛ inches (7.6 x 5.7 x 0.3 cm)
Polymer clay, vintage bottle cap pieces, nuts and bolts; color copy transfer
PHOTO © ARTIST

Leslie Blackford
Mad as March Hare, 2005
3 x 1 inches (7.6 x 2.5 cm)
Polymer clay, crystal; sculpted, sanded, buffed
PHOTO © JOHN WIDMAN

BASIC SAFETY GUIDELINES

- Once a tool has been used for polymer clay it should become designated and never used again to prepare food.

- Preheat your oven using a separate interior oven thermometer to calibrate the true temperature.

- Cure your clay in a well-ventilated area with open windows and other ventilation.

- Wear a dust mask when handling dry powders.

- Wash your hands often.

- Don't smoke or eat while working with polymer clay.

- Wear eye protection when cutting, carving, drilling, and polishing polymer clay.

- Remove loose jewelry and scarves, tie back your hair, and wear goggles while using a buffing wheel.

Leslie Blackford
Ancient Animal Relics, 2004
2½ x 1 inches (6.4 x 2.5 cm)
Polymer clay, jade, glass beads;
sculpted, sanded, buffed

PHOTO © TODD HOGDES

Jacqueline Lee
Japanese Maple Inro, 2001
5½ x 2¾ x 1½ inches
(5.5 x 2.75 x 1.5 cm)
Polymer clay, pulverized metals,
woven cord

PHOTO © DAN HAAB

SL Savarick
Hockney Inro, 2004
2½ x 3 x 1 inches (6.4 x 7.6 x
2.5 cm)
Polymer, silk cord; screenprinted

PHOTO © ROBERT DIAMANTE

CHOOSE FROM PROJECTS THAT RANGE FROM COLORFUL AND ABSTRACT TO SOPHISTICATED AND DETAILED. THESE IMAGINATIVE PIECES INCORPORATE A WIDE RANGE OF TECHNIQUES TO EXPRESS EACH ARTIST'S DISTINCT AESTHETIC. BEFORE YOU BEGIN, QUICKLY READ THROUGH THE PROJECT TO ASSESS ITS SKILL LEVEL. SOME OF THE MORE COMPLEX PROJECTS ARE FOUND LATER IN THIS CHAPTER. VARY THESE PIECES IN ANY WAY YOU LIKE TO DEVELOP YOUR OWN UNIQUE STYLE.

Crescendo Necklace

ARTIST

Judith Skinner

THIS NECKLACE
CONSISTS OF A
SERIES OF BEADS
IN GRADUATED
COLORS AND
SIZES, STRUNG
ON MEMORY
WIRE, WITH A
FINISHING SPIRAL
IN STERLING OR
GOLD-FILLED WIRE.
BECAUSE THE
WIRE CONFORMS
TO THE WEARER'S
NECK, NO CLASP
OR CLOSURE
IS NEEDED.

MATERIALS

Polymer clay: black, gold

50-grit emery cloth

Index cards

Memory wire

180-gauge floral wire

6 inches of 18-gauge half-hard wire:
 gold-filled, sterling, or copper

Seed beads, 6°

Cyanoacrylate glue

TOOLS

Pasta machine

Ruler

Tissue blade

Baking sheet

Pin vise with bits

Baking pan

Heavy-duty wire clippers

Needle-nose pliers

Flat-nose pliers

PROCESS

1. On the second thickest setting of your pasta machine, create a Skinner Blend from gold and black clay that measures about 10 inches long (photo 1 on page 26). Turn the sheet 90°, fold it, and run it through on the thickest setting of the pasta machine to stretch out the blend. You'll use about one block of each color.

2. Spray the 50-grit emery cloth with water to serve as a release agent. Place it next to the clay, and run them through the pasta machine. Allowing the two pieces to float freely as they run through will keep them from folding during the process. Immediately fold this sheet of clay lengthwise and place it back on the texture sheet. Use another texture sheet on top to gently press the fold flat, and press the two pieces together (photo 2 on page 26).

3. Square up both ends of the folded strip. Reserve the scrap from the darkest end for the tube beads. Place the ruler on the outside of a line that begins about 2¼ inches in from the edge and forms a diagonal line ending about ¼ inch from the edge. Cut the line with the tissue blade and cut the strip into 18 individual pieces, each about ½ inch wide (photo 3 on page 26).

4. As a reference point for drilling holes later, poke small holes on either side of each piece. Place the pieces facedown on index cards on top of a baking sheet. Bake the pieces at 275°F for about 45 minutes or according to the clay manufacturer's instructions. When you remove them from the oven, quickly place them face down on a cool surface and make sure they are flat.

(continued on page 26)

5. When they're cool, use the pin vise to drill holes large enough to hold the memory wire, but with a bit of slack. Drill into both sides to create clean holes.

6. Cut off two 6-inch pieces of floral wire. To make the tube beads, run a thin sheet of clay through the pasta machine and roll 5-inch tubes around each length of the wire until they are about ⅛ inch in diameter. Cut the clay so it's tapered where it will overlap and smooth the seam with your finger. Roll the clay over the texture sheet. Suspend the wires over a baking pan, and bake the clay. Remove the wire from the tubes as soon as you take them out of the oven. Immediately cut ½-inch-long beads at a right angle with the blade to give them the same sharp look as the beads (photo 4).

7. Use the heavy-duty wire clippers to cut a length from the coil of memory wire about three coils long (or 30 inches). (Avoid using wire cutters made for jewelry since the memory wire is spring steel and will do major damage to them.) Since the wire doesn't bend easily, hook a piece of 18-gauge sterling, gold-filled, or copper wire to each end of the memory wire. Drill the hole in the first piece slightly larger to allow the hooked wires to slip through and hide the join (photo 5).

8. String the graduated pieces on the memory wire, alternating them with seed beads. Add the tube beads last. Finish the final tube bead end with the same drilling technique as the starting piece. Add a bit of glue to secure the end pieces if they aren't tight.

9. When the necklace is fully assembled, use the pliers to form the wire into a decorative spiral.

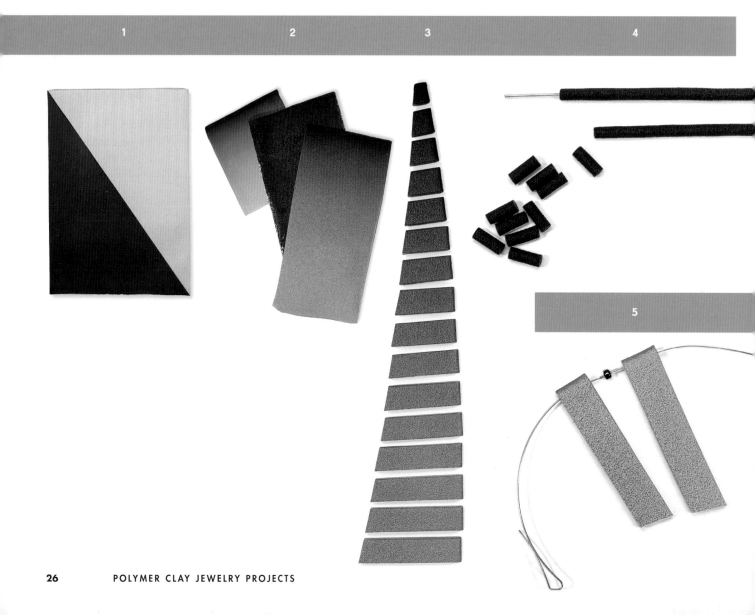

Bauhaus Necklace

ARTIST

Jacqueline Lee

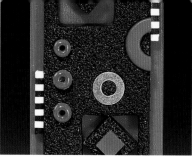

CLEAN LINES AND BITS OF HARDWARE CONTRIBUTE TO THE SUCCESS OF THIS SOPHISTICATED DESIGN. THE ARTIST FOLLOWS A "LESS IS MORE" AESTHETIC.

MATERIALS

Polymer clay: black, red, and white

100-grit sandpaper

Clear liquid polymer medium

3 red seed beads

1.6mm, M2, and 2.5mm flat washers

2-inch long piece of black wire

1/16-inch cable ferrule

18 inches of 1/32-inch galvanized cable

2mm hook-and-eye crimp clasp set

TOOLS

Pasta machine

Tissue blade

1/8, 1/4, and 3/4-inch square cutters

1/8 and 3/8-inch circle cutters

Wire cutters

Crimping tool

PROCESS

1. Roll out a sheet of conditioned black clay on the thickest setting of your pasta machine. Lay it on a small piece of sandpaper and roll it through again to texture one side.

2. Lay the sheet textured-side-up and use the tissue blade to cut out a rectangle. Use small square cutters to cut openings in the rectangle as shown (photo 1).

3. Roll out a very thin sheet of red clay. Cut two small circles out of the clay with the 3/8-inch circle cutter, and then use the 1/8-inch circle cutter to cut a centered hole out of one of the circles and an off-center hole from the other circle. Bake all of these cut pieces at 275°F for 10 minutes. Let them cool. Cut each of the holed circles in half (photo 2).

4. Coat one of each of the half-circular pieces and one of the small circles with a very thin coat of liquid medium. Place them on the black layer and press them gently to achieve a good bond. Add the seed beads and washers on the black layer (photo 3). Press gently so that they are slightly embedded in the clay. Bake this decorated layer at 275°F for 15 minutes, and then let it cool.

5. Roll out a sheet of red clay on the thickest setting. Place it on a small piece of sandpaper and roll it through again, on the same setting, to texture one side. Lay the clay, smooth side up, on a piece of sandpaper. Cut one edge with a tissue blade to make it perfectly straight; this will be the top edge.

6. Insert the piece of black wire into the cable ferrule and bend it. Lay the cable ferrule against the straight side of the red layer and press the bent wires into the clay (photo 4).

7. Score the backside of the decorated black layer and coat it with a thin layer of liquid medium. Press the piece onto the red background layer, centering it under the cable ferrule with the top edges even. Trim the red layer, leaving a border of 1/8 inch at both sides and across the bottom.

8. If the wire is visible in the top opening of the black layer, roll out a very thin sheet of red clay and cut out a square that is slightly smaller than the opening. Bake it for a few minutes to make it easy to handle and allow it to cool. Score the back lightly, coat with a thin layer of liquid medium and place it in the opening to cover the wire. Press gently to form a good bond.

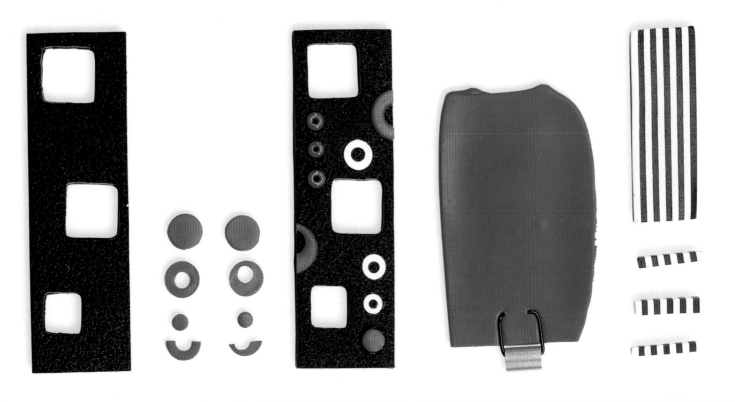

1	2	3	4	5

9. Use the sandpaper to create another small sheet of textured black clay on the thickest setting. Use the smallest circle cutter to cut out a tiny circle, a ⅛-inch square, and a ¼-inch square. Also cut a ⅛-inch square from a smooth, thin sheet of red clay. Bake these decorative elements for 10 minutes at 275°F and allow them to cool. Score the back of the decorative elements and coat them with a very thin layer of liquid medium. Turn the ⅛-inch black square on the diagonal and place it in the center of the top open square of the pendant. Press gently. Place the ¼-inch black square in the center of the middle open square and press it into place. Center the ⅛-inch red square on the ¼-inch black square and press lightly. Place the tiny black circle in the center of the bottom square opening and press gently. Bake the pendant on sandpaper for 15 minutes at 275°F or according to the clay manufacturer's suggestions.

10. Roll out a very thin sheet of black clay and a very thin sheet of white. Cut multiple squares from each sheet, and alternate them to form a striped stack. Use the tissue blade to slice a narrow piece off the stack. Trim the end of the striped slice to make it perfectly straight, and then cut off three small pieces, as shown, to use as decorative elements (photo 5).

11. Place the striped elements on the pendant as shown on page 27, and press gently. You can use a small amount of liquid medium between the pieces to ensure a strong bond. Bake the finished piece at 275°F for an hour. Allow it to cool off.

12. Feed one end of the galvanized cable through the cable ferrule. Place the clasp ends on the cable and use the crimping tool to firmly compress the middle section of the clasp ends.

Snakeskin Cuff Bracelet

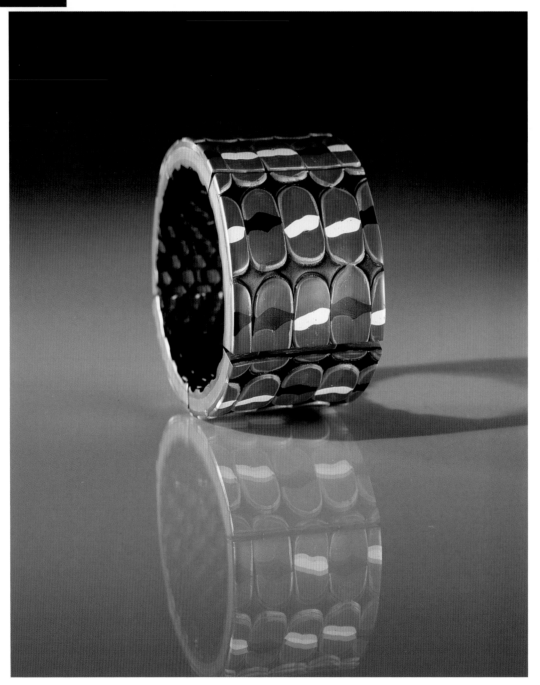

THE VENEER OF THIS FASHIONABLE BRACELET IS MADE FROM SLICES OF SIMPLE CANES COMPRESSED ON A BASE SHEET OF CLAY. THE RESULTING PATTERNING IS ORGANIC AND IMPERFECT, LENDING IT A NATURAL LOOK.

MATERIALS

Polymer clay: gold, black, and white

Glass bottle with a diameter of about 2½ inches

400- to 1500-grit sandpaper

TOOLS

Tissue blade

Transparent acrylic sheeting/thermo-plastic, approx. 2 x 8 inches

Pasta machine

Two bamboo sticks

Acrylic roller/brayer

Texture plate

Stretch black cord

PROCESS

1. Create a snake out of gold clay that is approximately 8 inches long and ½ inch thick. Use the tissue blade to cut it in half, forming two 4-inch pieces. Smooth each out by rolling it back and forth with the acrylic sheeting. Use the tissue blade to carefully slice each piece in half lengthwise.

2. Roll out some black clay on the thickest setting of your pasta machine. Place the flat side of one cut section of the gold snake on the black clay. Trim around it to produce a long black piece that matches it (photo 1 on page 32).

3. Place the other half of the gold strip on the other side of the black strip and work them together in a standard caning method, reducing it to a ⅜-inch diameter.

4. Roll out a sheet of white clay the same thickness as the black, and repeat this trimming and sandwiching process (photo 2 on page 32). Now you should now have two canes of equal diameter. Use the tissue blade to cut the canes into ⅛-inch slices.

5. Roll out a thin sheet of black clay that measures about 2½ x 8 inches. Arrange the slices on the sheet and roll it through the pasta machine on the thickest and then the next-to-thickest setting. Rolling this veneer is a bit tricky because it needs support on both ends to keep it straight.

6. Use a tissue blade to cut both of the canes into ⅛-inch slices. Place them in a pattern on the veneer (photo 3 on page 32). Roll the clay through on the thinnest and the next to thinnest settings on your pasta machine.

7. Make the bracelet's inner core by rolling out a sheet of gold clay on the thickest setting of your pasta machine. The piece should measure at least 2½ x 8½ inches. Place the two bamboo sticks parallel to one another and ¾ inch apart. Drape the clay lengthwise over the sticks. Use the acrylic roller to roll the clay over the sticks. Leave the sticks in place until you are ready to assemble the layers.

8. Roll a thin sheet of black clay twice on the same setting of your machine to form the interior layer of your bracelet. Roll it one more time on the same setting with a texture plate of your choice.

(continued on page 32)

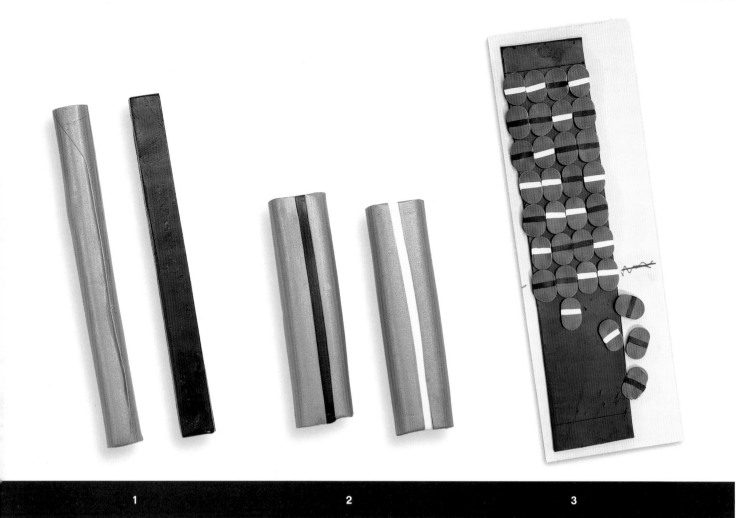

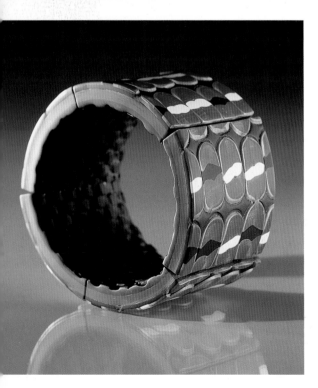

9. Remove the sticks and assemble the three layers (veneer, core, and interior). Trim them to a width of 1½ inches with a tissue blade. Lightly score the piece into five 1½-inch sections. Wrap it around a glass bottle with a diameter of about 2½ inches, trimming and butting the ends of the sandwiched clay as needed.

10. Cure the bracelet according to the clay manufacturer's specifications. Remove the piece from the oven, and while it is still warm, slice the scored sections with a tissue blade.

11. Begin with 400-grit sandpaper and work your way up to 1500-grit to sand and buff the bracelet.

12. Assemble it using stretch beading cord.

Etched Disc Necklace

ARTIST
Louise
Fischer Cozzi

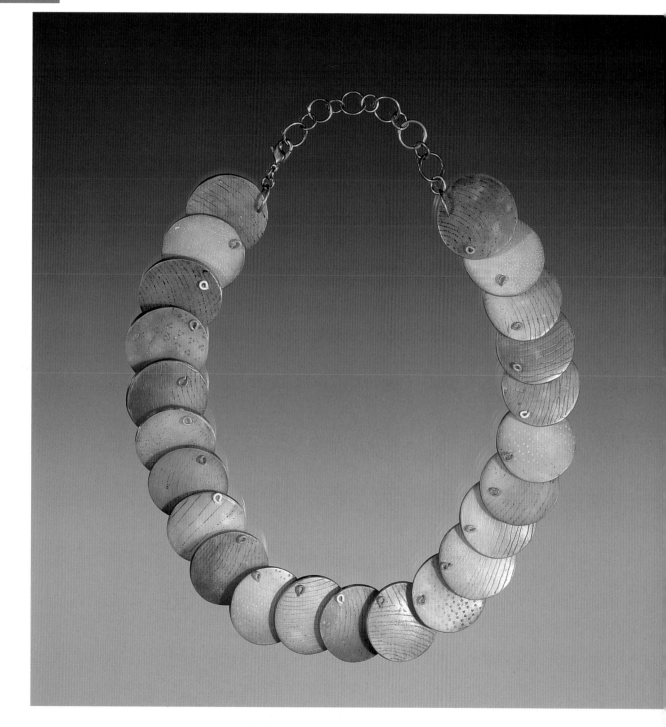

USE A TRANSFER METHOD AND ARTISTS' MEDIA TO CREATE THIS GORGEOUS NECKLACE OF OVERLAPPING COLORED DISCS THAT RESTS GRACEFULLY AROUND THE WEARER'S NECK. A SIMPLE TRANSFER ETCHING PROCESS, TAUGHT TO THE ARTIST BY GWEN GIBSON CREATES THE TEXTURED LOOK ON THE BEADS.

MATERIALS

Polymer clay: translucent

Black and white drawing/pattern photocopied onto a toner-based photocopy machine

Hemispherical slump mold (such as a floodlight in its cardboard package or a rounded lampshade)

Wet/dry sanding paper or pads (fine and extra-fine)

Gold-leafing pen

Cotton swabs

Oil paints in various colors

High-quality colored pencils

Soft rag

24-gauge colored craft wire in various colors

23 metallic Heishi beads (one for each clay bead)

Jump rings: 8 large, 6 small

Clasp

TOOLS

Acrylic roller

Pasta machine

Tissue blade

1-inch circle cutter

Pin vise

Round-nose pliers

2 pairs of chain-nose pliers

Wire cutters

PROCESS

1. Use the acrylic roller to flatten the clay before conditioning it on the second thickest setting on your pasta machine.

2. Place the photocopy of your drawing/pattern facedown on the clay, and burnish it. Allow it to sit for about eight minutes before burnishing again. Quickly rip off the paper. The image will be etched into the clay. The photocopy paper should feel raised and there will be little, if any, ink showing on the clay. You'll have an incised design (photo 1). Keep repeating this process on enough sheets of clay to provide you with 23 beads. (Note: All areas of your etchings may not be completely ink-free, some might end up with a bit of ink showing. You can still use these if you wish to add tonal variety to the work.)

3. Use the circle cutter to cut out at least 23 circles from the etched clay. Bake on the slump mold at 250°F for 30 minutes or as suggested by the clay manufacturer. Remove the discs from the oven and allow them to cool (photo 2).

4. Use the fine sandpaper or pads to sand the edges until they're smooth. Follow up with the extra-fine sandpaper. Use the gold-leafing pen to paint the edges of the beads with two coats,

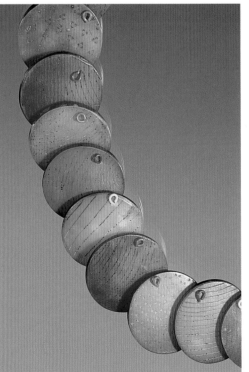

allowing the liquid to dry between coats (photo 3). Sand any excess gold off the back.

5. Use cotton swabs to paint the tops and backs of the beads with oil paints. Use two shades of oils on each bead, such as cadmium red and alizarin crimson or cadmium yellow light and sap green. Begin with the lighter color in the center and place darker colors around the edges (photo 4). Blend the colors with the tips of your fingers.

6. Swab each of the backs of the discs with a color of your choice. Clean up the gold edges with a cotton swab. Bake the discs in a 250°F oven for 15 minutes to dry the oil paint. When dry and cool, add more color to the pieces with matching colored pencils. Buff the discs with a soft cloth for a nice sheen.

7. Arrange the discs in an aesthetically pleasing way. Make sure there's a nice contrast between them; for instance, you might not choose to clump all the darks and lights together, but disperse them instead.

8. Using a pin vise, drill holes in the beads that are slightly larger in diameter than the craft wire, or approximately ⅛ inch in from both edges.

9. You'll connect the beads with small lengths of wire. Begin by cutting a short piece of one of the wires, and use the tip of the round-nose pliers to make a loop on one end of the wire. Use chain-nose pliers to turn this loop perpendicular to the rest of the wire. Insert the straight end of the wire through the bead so the loop rests on top of it (photo 5).

10. Slide a Heishi bead onto the straight end of the wire on the back of the bead. This bead serves as a washer between the beads. Thread the remaining wire through the top of next bead. Use the wire cutters to cut the wire to ¼ inch before looping it on the back of the adjoining bead. Press the loop with the cushioned handle of the pliers so it lies flat on the bead. Make sure the rough edge is not sticking out, but pointed towards the back of bead.

11. Continue adding beads with short pieces of colored wire until all of the beads have been connected. At either end of the necklace, make holes big enough for large jump rings. Use pliers to insert a large jump ring, and attach the clasp on the left-hand side of the finished side of necklace (if you are right handed). Reverse the placement if you're left handed.

12. To the other side of the clasp, add alternating large and small jump rings to form a chain of about 2 inches so the necklace's length is adjustable.

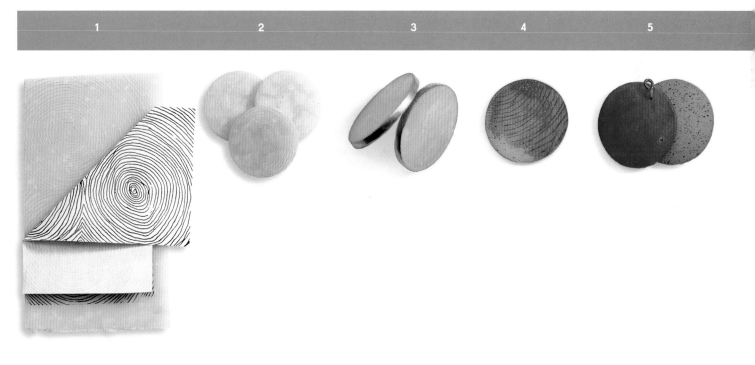

1   2   3   4   5

Flecked Triple-Chain Earrings

ARTIST
Louise
Fischer Cozzi

These earrings, whose surfaces resemble softly sparkling stones, are made with new and scrap clay combined with metallic leaf. The gentle curve on the beads is created by a slump mold.

MATERIALS

Polymer clay: translucent and black

Gold and silver leaf, 2 sheets each

Cardstock

Hemispherical slump mold (such as a floodlight in its cardboard package or a rounded lampshade)

Wet/dry sanding paper or pads (fine and superfine)

Gold-leafing pen

Silver-leafing pen

Eight ⅜-inch jump rings

Two ⅛-inch jump rings

2 niobium ear wires

TOOLS

Pasta machine

Dental or needle tool

Tissue blade

Teardrop-shaped canapé cutter

Pin vise with bits

2 pairs of chain-nose pliers

PROCESS

1. Condition about 1 ounce of translucent clay at the second widest setting on your pasta machine. Place the conditioned clay on top of the gold leaf and burnish it. Turn the piece over and add leaf to the other side of the clay. Run this clay through the pasta machine several times until it's thoroughly embedded in the clay (photo 1). Condition more translucent clay, this time adding a pea-sized amount of black clay to darken it. Then burnish the silver leaf onto this piece of clay and follow the same procedure that you used for the gold clay (photo 2).

2. Cut out the main earring shape from cardstock. Beginning with the gold clay, use the dental or needle tool to trace the shape on it once before flipping it over to trace a mirrored version of the shape. Cut out the shapes with a tissue blade. Use the teardrop cutter to cut out two more shapes from the remaining gold clay.

3. From the silver clay, trace the template twice and reverse it to cut out a total of four pieces.

4. In preparation for baking, place all of the larger pieces on a slightly curved slump. Place them in reverse positions, as seen in the final earrings. Place the two teardrop-shaped beads on a piece of cardboard or other flat surface. Bake the pieces at 250°F for 30 minutes. When cool, sand the edges until smooth, using fine and then extra-fine sanding pads (photo 3).

5. Use the gold-leafing pen to paint the edges of the gold pieces with two coats, and sand any excess gold off the backs of the pieces. Use the silver-leafing pen to paint the edges of the silver pieces with two coats and then sand the back.

6. Use a pin vise fitted with a bit to drill two central holes slightly bigger than the larger jump rings, each about ⅛ inch from the top and bottom of each piece.

7. Use a smaller drill bit to drill holes through the sides of the two teardrop beads to accommodate the smaller jump rings. Lay each teardrop bead on its side and carefully drill a hole about ⅛ inch from the tip of the bead. (Since this is a bit difficult, you might want to make extra beads to practice on.)

8. Use two pairs of pliers to open and close the jump rings as you assemble the earring. Add the ear wires.

| 1 | 2 | 3 |

Living in the Bronx Pin

THIS PIECE WAS INSPIRED BY LIGHT CASCADING OFF A MULTITUDE OF BUILDINGS, EMULATING THE URBAN LOOK OF THE BRONX. MICA SHIFT IS MADE POSSIBLE BY THE USE OF SILVER CLAY, CREATING THE PIN'S INTRIGUING SURFACE.

MATERIALS

Polymer clay: silver, white, orange (or blended color of your choice)

Pin back

TOOLS

Pasta machine

¼-inch square metal punch

Cane slicer

Texture plate

Tissue blade

PROCESS

1. Build a cane by stacking four 1½ x 1¾ x 1½-inch pieces of silver clay. Roll out a thick piece of white clay large enough to cover the top of the cane and cut it to fit.

2. With the white side of the clay facing up, use the square punch to punch through the white clay, straight down through the silver block. Remove the punch. Create a grid pattern by repeating this process to make punches in the clay (photo 1).

3. Use a cane slicer to remove the top white layer, revealing squares rimmed with white and a silver background. Slice thick layers of clay from the cane. Choose one of them to use as your pin top (photo 2).

4. Roll a thick sheet of orange clay (or other contrasting color) to serve as the pin's second layer. Place the pin top on this color along one of the rough edges created by the pasta machine (photo 3). Set it aside.

5. Roll out a piece of silver clay and roll it again with a texture plate to serve as the back layer for the pin. Sandwich the layers together and trim the edges with a tissue blade, leaving the contrasting rough edge showing.

6. Attach the pin back with clay (see page 20) and cure the piece according to the clay manufacturer's instructions.

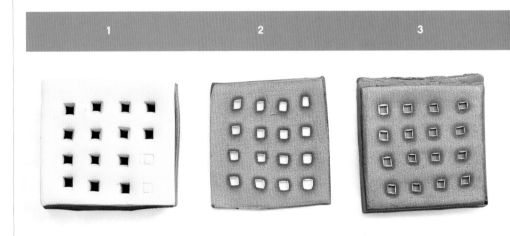

1

2

3

Slip Celadon Necklace

ARTIST

Mari O'Dell

TO CREATE A CELADON GLAZE WITH RAISED SLIP DESIGNS, PEARL AND TRANSLUCENT LIQUID POLYMERS ARE TINTED WITH ALCOHOL-BASED STAMPING INKS AND APPLIED TO CURED CLAY.

MATERIALS

Polymer clay: white, ecru, black, silver, and gold

Deli wrap

Latex gloves

Pearl and translucent liquid polymer

Alcohol-based rubber stamp inks (two shades of green)

20-gauge beading wire

Small glass spacer beads

Silver spacer beads

Sterling silver crimps

Silver clasp

TOOLS

Pasta machine

1-inch circle cutter

Tissue blade

Craft knife

Pro-bead roller #2

Pin tool

Several small-gauge metal knitting needles

Bead rack

Applicator squeeze bottle with #7 metal tip

Heat gun

Small soft brush

Wire cutters

Crimping tool

PROCESS

1. Combine the white clay with bits of ecru and a very tiny bit of black to create a color similar to old porcelain (photo 1). Condition the clay well. Roll a sheet of clay through the widest setting of the pasta machine.

2. Cut a central piece and two side panels from the sheet of clay. Set these aside on deli wrap.

3. Re-roll scraps of the clay into a smooth sheet on the widest setting of the pasta machine. Use the circle cutter to cut out fourteen 1-inch circles from the sheet. Use the craft knife to score the circle in quarters. Cut away one quarter. Roll the remaining three-quarters into 14 balls (photo 2).

(continued on page 42)

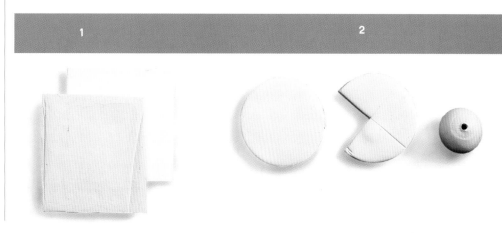

1

2

4. Use the pro-bead roller #2 to create 14 uniform and smooth beads. To avoid fingerprints on the beads, put on latex gloves to gently hold them when you pierce each with the pin tool.

5. Remove the beads from the pin tool, and widen each bead's hole by piercing it again with a small-gauge metal knitting needle. Space several beads on a series of needles and set them aside on a bead rack.

6. Fill the applicator bottle with pearl liquid polymer and place the tip on it. Test the flow of the liquid on a piece of paper. Apply a series of raised dots along the top of each bead. Set aside the bottle and move the heat gun over the beads to set the dots, changing their surface color slightly (photo 3). Turn the needle a bit to expose more of the beads, and continue adding dots and curing them. When all the beads are dotted, cure them in a preheated 275°F oven for 25 minutes.

7. While the beads are curing, trail designs with the same pearl polymer on the center and panel pieces. Cure the panels as you did the beads. Allow them to cool.

8. Pour about 2 tablespoons of pearl liquid polymer into a disposable cup, and 2 tablespoons of translucent liquid into a separate cup. Tint each liquid with a few drops of the green alcohol-based rubber stamp inks. Mix to achieve a color that you like. Use a brush to flow the tinted pearl polymer over both of the panels and the beads on the rack. Cure all the pieces again in a preheated 275°F oven for 25 minutes.

9. While the surface treatment is curing, create the backs for the three panels by mixing 1 ounce of silver polymer and ¼ ounce of gold polymer. Condition the clay well. Roll it out on the widest setting of the pasta machine before setting it aside on deli wrap. Save the scraps.

10. After the panels and central piece cool off, place them on top of the silver/gold sheet. Use the craft knife to trim around them so the tops are flush but the sides and bottom have ⅛-inch borders. Smooth the edges with your fingertips.

11. Cure the backed pieces at 275°F for 25 minutes. When cool, turn the panels and central piece over and use a pin

tool to score a channel ½ inch from the top of each piece. This channel will hold the wire. V-cut the channel with the craft knife. Place a small length of beading wire in each channel to make sure it is deep enough.

12. Roll the silver/gold clay scraps into a thin, smooth sheet. Cut a rectangular piece of clay to cover each channel, and smooth the edges (photo 4). Cure at 275°F for 20 minutes.

13. Use wire cutters to cut the beading wire slightly longer than you wish the finished necklace to be. Thread on the central piece with two glass spacer beads on either side. Add the accompanying panels, and place two silver spacers on either side of them. Slide on the dotted beads, sandwiched between spacers. When you run out of clay beads, add a series of spacers to fill the remaining wire.

14. Use a crimping tool to add silver crimp beads to each end of the wire. Add a sterling silver clasp.

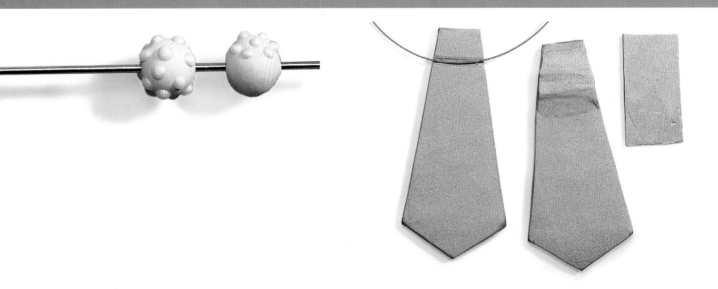

Calla Earrings

ARTIST

Judith Skinner

THE SIMPLE SHAPES OF THESE PIECES SHOW OFF THE BEAUTIFUL AND GRADUALLY SHIFTING COLORS OF A PEARLESCENT SKINNER BLEND. MAKE THE EARRINGS LONGER OR SHORTER TO SUIT YOUR TASTES.

MATERIALS

Polymer clay: red pearl, gold, blue pearl, opaque purple

Plastic wrap

Index cards

10 inches of 22-gauge half-hard wire (gold-filled or sterling)

Seed beads, 8°

Piece of scrap wire or dental floss

Pair of French ear wires

TOOLS

Pasta machine

Leaf-shaped cutter

Wire cutters

Metal file

Needle-nose and flat-nose pliers

PROCESS

1. Roll and cut the pieces of clay, as shown in photos 1 through 3, to create a rainbow Skinner Blend from red pearl, gold, blue pearl, and a purple mixed from equal parts of red pearl, blue pearl, and opaque purple.

2. Roll the blend into a thin sheet of clay on your pasta machine (photo 4). (At this thickness, a set of earrings with five pieces requires about a 5-inch length of clay.)

3. Place a sheet of plastic wrap over the clay to protect it, and use the leaf-shaped cutter to cut out shapes. When you use the cutter's plunger to remove the clay, the plastic wrap will keep it from making marks on the clay (photo 5). Smooth the edges of the shapes with your fingertips.

4. From scrap clay, make a small cone that's about 1½ inches tall and ¾ inches in diameter. Cure it. Wrap the cone gently around one of the clay shapes to create a dimensional shape, leaving a hole in the top about ⅛ inch in diameter. Overlap the edges of the shape (photo 6). Repeat this process, overlapping each shape in the same direction, to make as many shapes as you want to use for one earring (whether one, three, or five). Create the same number of shapes for the other earring, overlapping them in the opposite direction.

5. In preparation for curing, place the pieces on index cards to avoid marks from the baking surface. Cure the pieces at 275°F for about 30 minutes or according to the clay manufacturer's instructions. No sanding or buffing is needed when you are done, because the pearlescent clays have such a nice finish.

6. Next, use wire cutters to cut the 22-gauge wire into two pieces. If you're

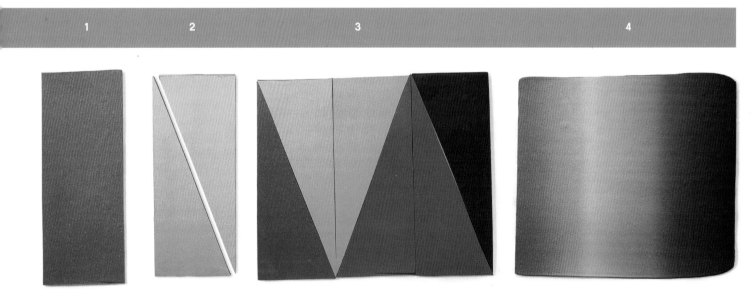

making single-piece earrings, cut two 3-inch pieces; for three-part earrings, cut two 4-inch pieces; and for five-part earrings, cut two 5-inch pieces. Smooth one end of each wire with a metal file.

7. Use the needle-nose pliers to form a tight spiral at one end of each of the wires. Thread about 10 seed beads onto each wire (photo 7). Slide the shaped pieces onto the wire to test their fit, and then mark the wire where they end at the top, i.e. where you'll make a loop for the ear wires. Remove the shaped pieces from the wire and use the flat-nose pliers to form the loop. Twist it a couple of times and cut off the excess wire. (You don't have to be extremely neat because the wrap will be hidden by the shaped pieces.)

8. Bend a piece of scrap wire or dental floss in half, and insert it in the loop to pull the wire and beads through the holes in the shaped pieces. Attach the loops to the French ear wires.

5

6

7

Art Nouveau Pendant

ARTIST

Mari O'Dell

THE DESIGN OF THIS PIECE WAS INSPIRED BY THE ARTIST'S FONDNESS FOR ART NOUVEAU ENAMELS. USE A DEEPLY ETCHED RUBBER STAMP AS YOUR TEXTURE PLATE TO CREATE THE EMBOSSED DESIGN.

MATERIALS

Polymer clay: gold, red pearl, green pearl, and black

Deli wrap

Coarse sandpaper

Liquid polymer, black

20-gauge gunmetal wire

Wide soft-glass rubber cording

Wide silver tension clasp

Permanent black ink

Cyanoacrylate glue

TOOLS

Pasta machine

Tissue blade

Craft knife

Spray bottle filled with water

Deeply etched rubber stamp (at least 3 inches square)

2 ¼-inch oval cutter

Old credit card

Ceramic tile

Pin tool with bits

Small-gauge metal knitting needle

Large-gauge metal knitting needle

Bead reamer

Coarse, medium, fine, and superfine sanding blocks

Water container

Buffing wheel with unsewn muslin buff

Polymer clay extruder with molding disc

Wire cutters

Two pairs of jewelry pliers

PROCESS

1. Create a well-conditioned Skinner Blend from gold, red pearl, and green pearl clay. Roll it into a sheet on the widest setting of the pasta machine and set it aside on deli wrap.

2. Place the rubber stamp face-up on the paper. Spray the sheet with water on the front and back before draping the clay over the stamp. Begin pressing in the center and out to the edges, making sure that the clay has good contact with the stamp. Lift the sheet off the stamp (photo 1 on page 48). Place the embossed sheet face-up on the deli wrap, and smooth out the clay as needed.

3. Use the oval cutter to cut a shape out of the textured sheet. Place this piece on the tile and cure it in a preheated 275°F oven for 25 minutes. Allow it to cool.

4. Fill in the pressed areas with black liquid polymer and level it by drawing an old credit card across the surface. Clean off excess black liquid from the raised areas (photo 2 on page 48). (The more excess you remove, the less sanding you'll need to do later.) Cure in a preheated 275°F oven for 25 minutes. Allow the pendant to cool.

(continued on page 48)

5. Form a bead from the scraps of the Skinner Blend and black clay to place below the oval piece. Use a sharp tool to puncture the surface of the colored clay, leaving dots. Pierce the bead with the pin tool. Cure the bead for 20 minutes at 275°F and backfill the holes with black liquid polymer. Cure again for 10 minutes, and allow the bead to cool.

6. When the oval and bead cool off, fill the bucket with water, and sand them in water, beginning with the coarse block and ending with the superfine one. Change the water between grits. Dry off the oval and the bead. Buff both to a high shine and set them aside.

7. Set the pasta machine to a medium thickness, and roll out a sheet of well-conditioned black clay that is large enough to encompass the oval. Press coarse sandpaper over the sheet to create texture (photo 3). Place the textured side down on deli wrap. Place the buffed oval on top of the smooth side of the textured sheet and use a craft knife to trim it to the shape of the oval. Press the sheets together.

8. Roll out a well-conditioned piece of black clay and prepare a log. Fill the extruder and set the molding disc to smoothly extrude a bezel to surround the oval (photo 4). Gently fit the piece around the oval and press it in place to form a bezel. Trim the ends so that the two pieces butt together at the top of the piece.

9. To make the top textured bead (the bail), form a thick tube bead and leave it on the needle before pressing it onto the textured stamp. Texture the entire bead, rolling it gently to reshape and widen the hole (photo 5).

10. Press the bead into the top of bezel and trim off the excess clay. Cap the ends of it with discs cut or punched from both colored and black polymer which has been rolled into a sheet on the thickest setting of the pasta machine.

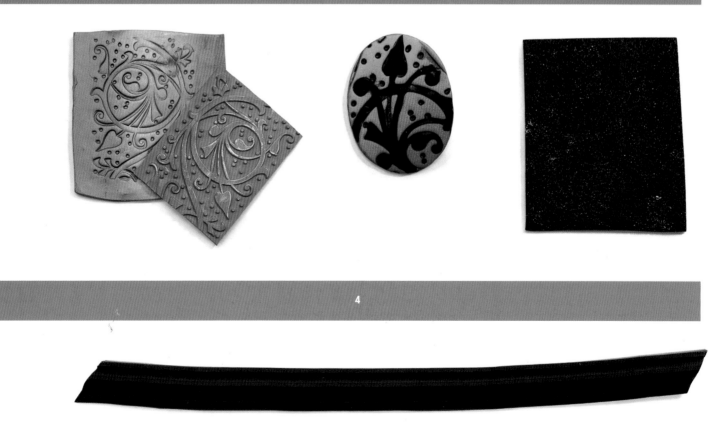

1

2

3

4

11. Cure in a preheated 275° oven for 25 minutes. Allow the piece to cool. Sand the tube bead and caps and buff them.

12. Use jewelry pliers to form a small spiral with the gunmetal wire. Wrap one end of the wire around one pair of pliers, while you hold the wire in place with the other pair. When you're done, thread the end of the wire through the small bead and bend the wire as it comes out of the bead (photo 6). At the bottom of the pendant, lay the crimped wire against the bezel back and cover it with a thin sheet of textured black clay. Smooth the edges and retexture the clay. On top of the wire, add a flattened bead of black clay to prevent movement of the bead and wire.

13. Use a craft knife to widen the holes in the black textured tube, and use a bead reamer to smooth the hole and widen it further so the soft-glass rubber cording fits inside of it. Cut off a piece of cording slightly longer than you wish the necklace to be. Coat the inside of the holes of the tube bead with the glue and work the cording into them. Allow the glue to dry. Cut the cording into two equal lengths that meet directly across from the pendant.

14. Place the silver tension clasp in place and check the length again, adjusting as needed. Brush permanent black ink on it and allow it to dry before wiping the surface off, leaving the ink in the grooves.

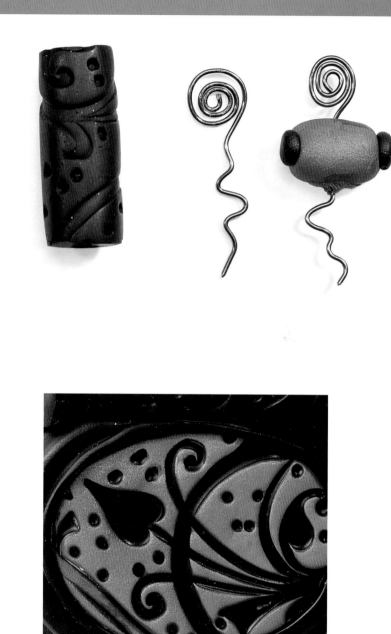

Souvenir Bracelet

ARTIST

Mari O'Dell

A SOUVENIR IS A TOKEN OF REMEMBRANCE OR A MEMENTO. THIS BRACELET IS A CLEVER WAY TO DOCUMENT ANY EVENT. IT COMBINES PHOTOGRAPHY, CLAY, RUBBERSTAMPING MATERIALS, AND COMPUTER TECHNOLOGY.

MATERIALS

Polymer clay: black and white

Photos

Inkjet waterslide decal paper

Deli wrap

Heavy paper or quilter's template

Black beading elastic

Soft wedge-shaped sponge

Paper towels

Piece of cardboard

Rubber stamp images

Cyanoacrylate glue

Small black spacer beads

Large black decorative bead for closure (about ½ inch wide)

Heat–set ink for stamping

Fine embossing powder, clear

TOOLS

Computer, scanner, and inkjet printer

Scissors or craft knife

Pasta machine

Large-gauge knitting needle

Tissue blade

Ruler

Plastic spoon

Curing tile

Metal needle tool

Pin vise with bits

Toothpick

PROCESS

1. Gather favorite photos, preferably all of the same size/format. Choose ones with clear, bold images that have well-defined edges (photo 1). Scan the images and reduce them before printing them out on an inkjet printer. Assuming you're using rectangular photos, your end goal is to end up with small images measuring about 1 x ¾ inches each (photo 2).

2. Transfer the sheet of images onto waterslide decal paper according to the manufacturer's instructions. Allow the printed images to rest for several hours.

3. Use scissors or a craft knife to trim the images. Roll out a piece of well-conditioned black polymer clay on the widest setting of your pasta machine and place it on a piece of deli wrap for ease of handling. Trim to a piece that measures 2 x 7 inches. Cut this piece in half lengthwise so you have two identical pieces of clay, each measuring 1 x 7 inches. Set aside one of the black pieces for later.

4. Cut a piece of heavy paper or a quilter's template into a ½-inch-wide and 7-inch-long piece. Use scissors to cut a small notch in the center of each end of this first template. From the same material, cut out another rectangle for the bracelet that measures 1 x 7 inches. Place the narrower template on top and in the center of the wider one, and cut two notches in the wider template that match.

5. Place the narrower template in the center of the black clay strip, and cut away the notches from the clay with your craft knife. Drag the knitting needle slowly and carefully along either side of the template to form smooth, straight channels. This process should take several pulls. Since the channel must hold the beading elastic and will serve as the bead's hole later, check the depth of the channel with a length of it to make certain it fits.

6. Roll out a thin, non-wrinkled sheet of well-conditioned white polymer clay and cut a 1 x 7-inch piece from it. Carefully position the white clay sheet on top of the extra piece of black clay that you cut in step 3. Smooth it to prevent trapping any air bubbles.

7. Roll these sandwiched sheets lengthwise through the pasta machine on its widest setting. Because the clay will now be larger after rolling, place the bracelet template on the sandwiched piece, and trim around the edges. Cut out the notches too. Place this trimmed piece over the channeled strip of black clay with the white side up. Trim the sides to make them even (photo 3).

8. Place one of the trimmed decals into a small bowl of water. When they begin to slide off the backing, carefully slide it onto the white polymer tile backing. Use a soft, wedge-shaped sponge to work out any air bubbles and pat the decals dry with a paper towel. Trim the edges

of the tile with a tissue blade (photo 4), and place it on a curing tile or card. Create seven tiles and cure them in a preheated 275°F oven for 30 minutes or follow the suggestions of the clay manufacturer. Allow them to cool.

9. Turn the tiles over and stamp the backs with a rubberstamp and heat-set ink. Place the tiles on a piece of plain cardboard with the stamped image against the cardboard. Cure for 10 minutes in a preheated 275°F oven. Allow the tiles to cool.

10. Place embossing powder in the spoon and use it to gently sift a coating of clear embossing powder over the photo decal images. Wipe off the sides of the tiles. Place them on a curing tile in a preheated 275°F oven until the powder is liquid and clear (photo 5).

When you remove the tiles from the oven, be careful not to tip the curing tile since the embossing powder is still liquid and can run.

11. If you see small bubbles on the surface, touch them with the tip of a metal needle tool before the tiles cool. (After the first coating, you can add more embossing powder and cure the tiles again, if you wish.)

12. Cut the beading elastic to 2½ times the length needed for your bracelet (the bracelet shown measures 6 inches). Coat each end of the elastic with glue to stiffen the tips.

13. Check the tiles for smooth edges and clear the holes. Sand the edges or re-drill the holes as needed. String six spacer beads onto the beading elastic to

form the loop closure. Bend the elastic into a curve with equal lengths on either side in preparation for stringing the tiles. String on the first tile and snug it up to the beads. String the stiff ends of the elastic through the holes in each of the seven tiles, adding spacer beads between each.

14. Ad two final spacer beads, then stretch and knot the two pieces of elastic several times. String both ends of the elastic through the closure bead and knot it several times. Pull the knot away from the larger bead, and use a toothpick to dot the hole with glue. Push the knot back into the bead hole. Dab the hole with more glue. Allow it to dry and clip away any extra elastic.

3

4

5

Galaxy Bead Necklace

ARTIST

Jennifer Bezingue

GLASS ARTISTS AND JEWELRY MAKERS ARE OFTEN INTRIGUED BY THE FACT THAT GLASS-LIKE BEADS CAN BE MADE FROM POLYMER CLAY. TECHNIQUES SUCH AS THIS UNDERSCORE ADVANCES IN THE MEDIUM.

MATERIALS

Polymer clay: pearlescent, darker clays of your choice, translucent

Waxed paper

Opaque polyester glitter

Mica powder

Polyester fiberfill

Wet/dry sandpaper in range of coarsest to finest grits (220 to 2000)

49-strand beading wire

Colored glass beads

Sterling silver beads and bead caps

Sterling silver tube crimp beads

Sterling silver toggle clasp

TOOLS

Pasta machine

Miniature shape cutters

Craft knife

Needle tool

Baking sheet

Safety glasses

Electric buffing machine with unstitched muslin wheel

Crimping pliers

Wire cutters

PROCESS

1. To create the base bead, form a ¾ to 1-inch ball of clay by mixing pearlescent and darker clays together.

2. Use the pasta machine to roll out a thin sheet of translucent clay. Smooth the sheet onto a layer of waxed paper, and pour small piles of opaque glitter on it. Rub the glitter evenly into the sheet. Shake off any excess glitter and place the sheet on waxed paper, with the glitter side facing up.

3. To create a mica-powder sheet, roll out a ½-inch ball of the translucent clay. Mix in the powder until the clay is stiff, and roll it out on a thin setting.

(continued on page 56)

4. Using miniature shape cutters and craft knife, cut pieces from the glitter sheet and lift them up carefully with the craft knife before placing them glitter-side-down on the base bead. Next, use the shape cutters and craft knife to cut out shapes from the mica-laden sheet. Place them on the base bead (photo 1). Press the appliqués firmly into the bead until they are level with the surface. Cover half to three-quarters of the bead with both types of appliqués.

TIP: When placing the appliqués on the beads, connect the design elements and create groupings of shapes. Try not to create organized patterns—random placement and a mix of colors will add up to a spontaneous design, full of life and movement.

5. Roll the base bead until the appliqués are fully incorporated into the surface, with no seams visible between the translucent and colored clay. Add a second layer of appliqués, pressing them into the surface of the bead, and overlapping them as you wish. When you're finished adding the appliqués, roll the surface until it's smooth and even, with no seams around the appliqués.

6. To shape the bead, place it in the palm of your hand with the best side facing up. Gently press down on the bead with your other palm, turning the bead, and flipping it over as you press each time. This will help you achieve a flattened and rounded piece with a slightly domed surface on each side.

7. Use the needle tool to make a hole through the bead. Repeat this process to create as many beads as you wish.

8. Bake the beads for 45 minutes at 275°F on a layer of polyester fiberfill atop the baking sheet. When the beads are fully baked, remove them from the oven and quench them in cold water to minimize cracking (photo 2).

9. When the beads are cool enough to handle, tear various grits of wet/dry sandpaper sheets into quarters. Put one piece of each into warm water for a few minutes until saturated. Begin hand sanding with the coarsest (220 grit) paper. Sand the bead's surface until it's smooth and the glitter appliqués come into sharp focus. If needed, spot-sand the appliqués that are less clear. When the bead is smooth, continue sanding it with the successive grits of sandpaper until you reach the finest grit (photo 3).

10. Put on your safety glasses and buff the bead at medium speed until the surface is glass-like.

11. In a design of your choice, string the larger beads onto the beading wire with smaller glass beads, sterling silver beads, and sterling beads caps between them. On each end of the wire, string a crimp bead and one end of the toggle. Bring the beading wire back through the crimp bead. Use crimping pliers to close the crimp bead and trim the beading wire beneath the bead.

1   2   3

Satin Pillows Necklace

ARTISTS

Pier & Penina

THE IDEA FOR THIS NECKLACE EVOLVED FROM CREATING VENEERS RESEMBLING FABRIC. THE VENEER IS THEN ROLLED OVER A CORE BEAD, AND THE ENDS PINCHED TO CREATE A SOFT LOOK.

MATERIALS

Polymer clay: gold and black blended to create bronze

Acrylic paint: blend iridescent gold, fine gold, and copper

Bead caps

Translucent liquid clay

³⁄₃₂ Buna rubber cord, 1 yard

Spacer beads

4 black rubber #004 o-rings

TOOLS

Pasta machine

Screenprinting stencil in pattern of your choice made with pre-emulsion screen stencil film (follow the manufacturer's instructions to make the stencil)

Squeegee (you can use an old credit card, if you wish)

Bead roller

Needle tool

Wooden skewer

Wavy-edged blade (available through kitchen suppliers)

Long metal knitting needles

Clay extruder and discs

Metal roasting pan

Pin vise with bits

PROCESS

1. Blend together two parts of the gold clay and one part of the black clay to roll a bronze-colored clay. Condition and produce about five sheets of clay on the next-to-thinnest setting on your pasta machine. Each sheet should measure about 3 x 8 inches.

2. Follow the instructions that come with your silkscreening film to transfer an image and make a stencil. Place the stencil, emulsion-side down, on a sheet of clay. Depending on the dimensions of the stencil, you may want to place it horizontally or vertically on the clay to get the most use out of the clay.

3. Mix the gold and copper acrylic paints to create a color that contrasts nicely with the clay. You'll need about 4 tablespoons of paint for the screening. Use the squeegee to place an even ribbon of paint along the shortest edge of the screen. Use the squeegee to draw the paint across the surface of the screen and clay. Apply a consistent pressure to ensure consistent coverage (photo 1). (You can use the same screen two or three more times on more clay before the screen becomes clogged and has to be washed. When it does, use warm water to gently loosen the paint from the non-emulsion side of the screen before rinsing and drying it.)

4. Use the bead roller and some scrap clay to make ½-inch diameter core beads. (The number is dependent on how long you want the necklace to be, but you should end up with an odd number of beads to ensure a nice drape when finished). Use your fingers to square off the edges of each bead.

5. From the screened clay, cut strips wide enough to cover the ends of each of the beads with about a ³⁄₈-inch extension on either side of the bead (or 1-inch wide strips), and long enough to wrap around them around the bead once with a slight overlap (about 2 inches).

6. Pierce the center of each bead with the needle tool. Remove the needle tool and carefully use that small hole to guide the bead core on a wooden skewer. (The wood keeps the bead from moving around during the next step.)

7. Wrap the strips of veneer made in step 5 around each bead core and use the wavy-edged blade to trim and finish each strip. Press gently to the bead and press the edges down around the bead holes, just up to the edge of the hole (photo 2). The beads don't have to be perfectly uniform—you'll be using bead caps to cover the rough edges.

8. Carefully guide the beads onto thin knitting needles, and suspend the needles over a roasting pan. Partially cure them for 20 minutes at around 275°F or a temperature designated by the clay manufacturer. Allow the beads to cool before applying the bead caps.

9. Use the extruder and discs to form a spaghetti-sized width of gold clay and a linguini-sized width made from bronze clay. Center the gold clay on top of the bronze clay to make a ribbon. Wind a short length of the clay ribbon (allow some overlap to make it interesting) around a small cylindrical object, such as a knitting needle. The diameter of the cap should be large enough to ensure that the bead cap, once removed from the needle, can sit around the bead hole and not obstruct it.

10. Use a bit of translucent clay to attach the bead caps made from the extruded ribbons (photo 3).

11. Cure the beads again for 15 minutes at 275°F or the temperature suggested by the manufacturer. Allow them to cool and then string the clay beads on a length of rubber cord, adding spacer beads of your choice between them. (The rubber cord should be 4 inches longer than the desired finished length so that you can leave 2 inches on each side that can be used to form the clasp.)

12. To make the clasp from clay beads and the rubber cord, form two small square beads wide enough to accommodate the rubber cord when doubled (or about $1/4$ inch long by $1/8$ inch wide) as well as a longer bead wide enough to fill the clasp and accommodate a single strand of rubber (about $1/2$ inch long by $1/4$ inch wide). Use the pin vise to drill the cord holes in the beads.

13. Pull one of the ends of the cord through one of the small cube beads, thread two o-rings onto it, and make a $1/2$-inch loop with the cord that you then secure by running the end of it back through the two o-rings. Snip the end of the cord just enough to be tucked back into the small square bead, keeping it covered. On the other side, do the same thing, with the exception of threading the larger rectangular bead on the cord before running the end back through the o-rings.

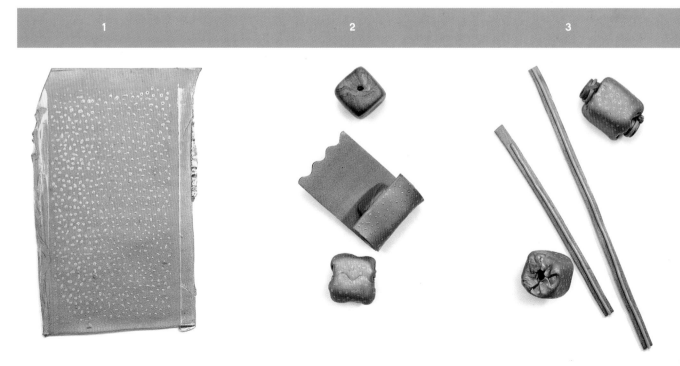

Japanese Kanji Necklace

ARTIST

Jacqueline Lee

A JAPANESE PICTOGRAM IS PORTRAYED ON THIS INTRICATE PENDANT. STAMPED CLAY, TOGETHER WITH GOLD LEAF, MAKES A WONDERFUL IMPRESSION.

MATERIALS

Polymer clay: black and metallic copper

Black pendant cord, 1 yard

Cyanoacrylate glue

Unlined paper or cardstock (to bake on)

Gold bronzing powder

Sheet of gold leaf

Clear liquid polymer

100-grit sandpaper

2 gold eye pins, each ½ inch long

Black crochet thread, 10 inches

Black horn hairpipe bead, ½ inch long

TOOLS

Pasta machine

Kanji rubberstamp

Dust mask

1⅛-inch circle cutter

Tissue blade

Oriental writing rubberstamp

2 small pairs of pliers

Small pair of wire cutters

PROCESS

1. Coat 1 inch of each end of the pendant cord with cyanoacrylate glue and hang to dry. The glue will stiffen the ends of the cord and make it easier to thread it through the beads.

2. Roll out a fairly thick sheet of black clay. Place the sheet of clay on a piece of unlined paper or cardstock.

3. Press the Kanji stamp into some scrap clay several times to make the surface tacky. Wearing a dust mask, pick up a small amount of gold bronzing powder on your finger and rub it carefully over the surface of the stamp. (Coat the surface well without getting the powder on the sides of the stamp, or your impression will look sloppy.) Stamp the sheet of clay with the coated stamp. You might need to do this several times.

4. Use the circle cutter to cut out the stamped Kanji. Pull away the excess clay (leaving the Kanji on the paper) and bake it at 275°F for 15 minutes.

5. Roll out a sheet of copper clay of a medium thickness. Trim the clay to the approximate size of the gold leaf and lay the clay on the leaf (this is easier than trying to apply the leaf to the clay). Run the leafed clay back through the pasta machine on the same setting to make certain the leaf is adhered well.

6. Adjust your pasta machine once again, this time to the next smaller setting, and run the clay through again. Decrease the setting one more time and turn the clay ¼ turn before running it through. Use the tissue blade to cut out a 1¼-inch square from this clay.

(continued on page 62)

| 1 | 2 | 3 |

7. Score the back of the baked Kanji piece with the tip of your craft knife, and coat it with a thin layer of liquid medium. Center the Kanji piece on the leafed square and press gently to form a good bond (photo 1). Bake the piece at 275°F for 15 minutes. Allow it to cool off.

8. Roll out a sheet of black clay the same thickness as the clay you used in step 3. Using the technique described earlier, coat the surface of the oriental writing stamp with gold bronzing powder and press it onto the sheet of clay (photo 2).

9. Score the back of the assembled Kanji/gold leaf layer. Coat it very lightly with liquid medium. Press this baked layer onto the unbaked stamped sheet. Trim the unbaked clay flush with the sides of the gold leafed square, leaving a $\frac{3}{16}$-inch border of the writing layer visible at the top and the bottom (photo 3). Bake the piece at 275°F for 15 minutes.

10. Roll out a medium-thickness sheet of metallic copper clay. Place it on a piece of sandpaper and roll it through again on the same setting to texture one side. Lay the clay, smooth-side-up, on a piece of sandpaper. Cut one edge with a tissue blade to make it perfectly straight; this will serve as the top edge of the pendant.

11. Hold an eye pin by the eye with a small pair of pliers. Use the second pair of pliers to bend the lower portion of the eye pin at a sharp angle. This bend will serve to anchor the eye pin in place so it won't pull free. Repeat with the second eye pin. Press the eye pins into the trimmed side of the copper layer, about $\frac{1}{2}$ to $\frac{3}{4}$-inch apart, with the eyes of the pins protruding above the edge of the clay (photo 4).

12. When the layered Kanji piece has cooled, turn it over and repeat the scoring and liquid medium process described in step 9. Press it firmly onto the metallic copper layer with the eye pins centered at the top and about $\frac{1}{16}$ inch of the copper layer visible. Trim the bottom edge to a $\frac{1}{16}$-inch border. Trim the sides of the bottom layer flush with the baked layer. Set the piece aside.

13. To make a clay hairpipe bead, form a small cylinder of black clay and insert a toothpick through it. Lay the cylinder on a flat surface and roll it back and forth until the clay spreads across the length of the toothpick (photo 5). Apply a bit more pressure at either end of the bead so that the ends will be slightly narrower than the middle. Trim the ends of the bead by placing the tissue blade at the desired spot and rolling it just as you did to shape it. Set the bead aside.

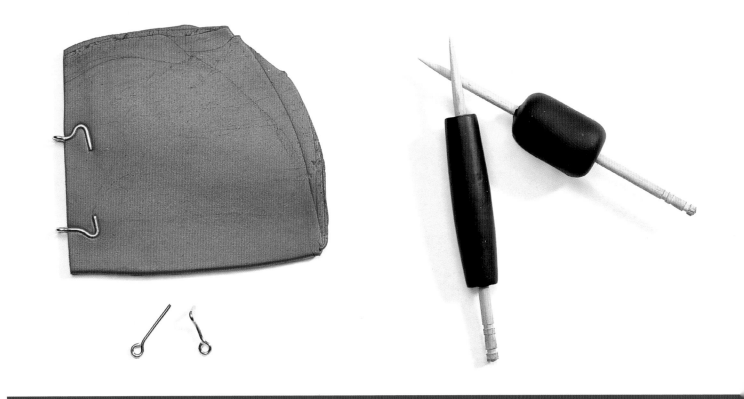

14. To make a gold-leafed bead for the top of the pendant, roll some of the excess leafed clay (leaf-side-out) into an 8 to 10 mm ball. Lay the ball on a flat surface and flatten into a roundel shape. Use a toothpick or a needle tool to make a hole in the center of the roundel. The hole should be large enough to accommodate a double thickness of your pendant cord.

15. Bake the hairpipe and gold-leafed beads along with the pendant for an hour at 275°F. Allow them to cool before removing the toothpick from the hairpipe. To do this, you might need to grasp the end with a pair of pliers and twist gently while pulling.

16. To tie the hairpipe bead to the pendant, cut the length of black crochet thread in half. Lay the pendant face down, and fold one of the lengths in half. Hold the ends of the thread together and thread them through the eye

(from the middle of the pendant out), so that you are left with a dime-sized loop of thread in the center and two long ends sticking out from the side.

17. Insert the hairpipe bead in the loop and center it across the top edge of the pendant. Bring one of the thread ends around the front of the bead and one around the back. Pull the loop snugly against the bead and tie the thread into a knot on the backside of the bead. Repeat on the other side. Dab a small amount of glue onto each knot to hold it in place. When dry, trim the ends of the thread flush with the knot.

18. Fold the necklace cord in half. Holding it at the loop end, thread it loop first (going in at the front of the pendant and out at the back) between the eye pins beneath the hairpipe bead until you have a loop of about 1½ inches at the back.

19. Fold the loop up (perpendicular to the hairpipe bead) and, holding the cord ends together, thread them through the loop and pull snug to form a lark's head knot around the bead.

20. Use sharp scissors to clip the dry stiffened ends of the pendant cord at a sharp angle. Thread the ends of the cord, one at a time, through the gold leafed bead and slide the bead down until it rests on the lark's head knot.

21. Thread the ends of the cord, one at a time, through the ½-inch horn hairpipe bead. The cord should fit snugly in the bead so that when the ends of the cord are pulled to adjust the length it will be held securely in place.

22. Tie a knot in the cord ends. Place a tiny dot of glue on the knots to secure them. When dry, trim the excess cord flush with the knot.

Mica Shift Circles Pendant

A PROCESS CALLED MICA SHIFT CREATES THE BEAUTIFUL SURFACE EFFECTS THAT YOU SEE ON THIS PENDANT. THE USE OF SILVER CLAY CONTAINING BITS OF MICA MAKES THIS POSSIBLE.

MATERIALS

Polymer clay: silver, black,
  burnt sienna, white

TOOLS

Pasta machine

Circle cutter set

⅛-inch round punch

Cane slicer

Texture screen

Tissue blades

#7 knitting needle

PROCESS

1. Mix silver clay with a bit of black and burnt sienna to achieve a bronze color, keeping in mind that there should be more silver in proportion to the other clays. This proportion will assure that the mica shift effect occurs.

2. Roll out the clay on the thickest setting on your pasta machine, and cut four rectangles from it measuring approximately 1½ x 2½ inches. Stack them to form a cane.

(continued on page 66)

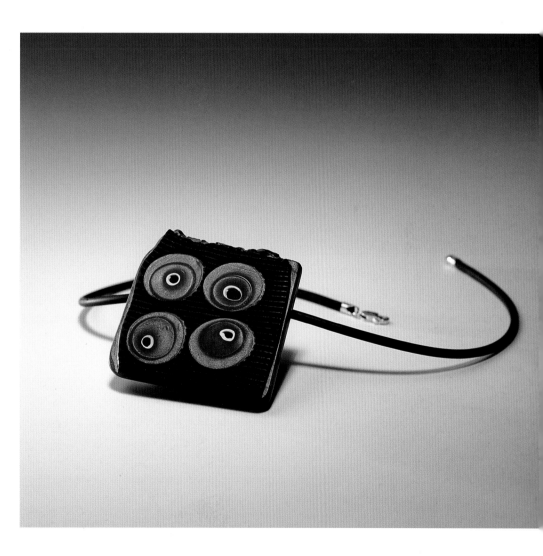

3. Use the larger circle cutter to carefully cut through the clay on ¼ of the cane, twirling it so it doesn't stick. Carefully pull it out to avoid removing any clay. Use a smaller cutter to cut another circle inside the first, following the same procedure. Repeat this to create the three remaining circular designs (photo 1).

4. After the cuts are made, gently press the clay back together, healing them without distorting the circles. Press just enough to remove air space created by the cut.

5. Roll out a small piece of white clay on the thickest setting of your pasta machine. Cut four ¼-inch squares from the clay. Place each square in the center of one of the circles, where you'll cut the smallest circle.

6. Use a ⅛-inch solid round punch to cut down through the white clay to the bottom of the silver clay, creating a hole in the center circle lined with white clay (photo 2).

7. Slice off the top layer with the cane slicer to remove the white clay on top and create an even surface for a subsequent slice.

8. Use the cane slicer to make clean slices from the top. Punch out the circles using the largest circle cutter, or one a bit larger than your largest punched circle (photo 3).

9. To create a background for the cut circles, roll out a sheet of medium-thickness black clay. Run the clay back through the machine with the texture screen.

10. Place the cut circles on the textured black background and run it back through the machine again to distort the circles slightly and adhere them to the textured surface.

11. Roll out a thick sheet of the bronze-colored clay for the center section of the piece, and cut three sides of it slightly larger than your finished piece, leaving one edge rough.

12. Use the texture plate to texturize a third layer of clay for the back of the piece.

13. Assemble the three layers together and trim the edges with a tissue blade.

14. Cure the piece according to the clay manufacturer's specifications.

15. Use black clay to create a tube approximately ¾ inch long by rolling it around a thick knitting needle. Roll it back and forth until smooth. The wall of the tube should be thick enough to retain its strength after it's baked. Remove from the needle and trim the tube's edges.

16. Place it on the back of the pendant and cure the piece again.

1   2   3

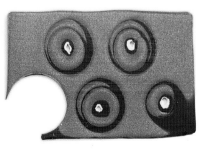

Log Cabin Quilt Pins

ARTIST

Judith Skinner

QUILT PATTERNS ARE EASILY ADAPTED TO POLYMER CLAY CANEWORK. THE CANE DESCRIBED HERE IS IN KEEPING WITH THE ACTUAL CONSTRUCTION OF A LOG CABIN QUILT BLOCK. BLACK LINES SEPARATE THE COLORS IN THE PATTERN, MAKING THE DESIGN MORE VISIBLE.

MATERIALS

Polymer clay: black, alizarin crimson, ultramarine, navy blue, sap green, ecru, white*

2 sheets of thin plastic wrap (to form a draped piece)

Pin backs

Blank index cards

TOOLS

Pasta machine

Tissue blade

Acrylic brayer

■ *The initial cane is about 2 x 4 inches and requires the equivalent of almost two clay blocks for each shade of blue and a small amount of red clay. You'll use at least a block of black clay, possibly two, depending on your pasta machine.*

PROCESS

1. To make the cane, you'll need clay in two dark colors, two light colors, red for the center, and black for the separation line. A monochromatic color scheme makes the project easier to plan. If you want to mix the exact colors shown here, they are:

> Navy= 3 parts ultramarine + 1 part navy blue + ¼ part sap green

> Ivory (for mixing) = 1 part ecru + 1 part white

Then use your navy and ivory mixes to create the remaining three blues:

> Dark blue= 5 parts navy + 3 parts ivory

> Medium blue= 3 parts navy + 5 parts ivory

> Light blue= 1 part navy + 4 parts ivory

To make the red center:

> 2 parts alizarin crimson + 1 part ivory

2. Mix the colors of clay and evaluate the settings on your pasta machine before rolling out sheets for the cane. If it produces a ⅛-inch thick sheet on the widest setting, use the second widest setting to prepare the colored sheets. If it doesn't have this wide of a setting, set it at the widest one possible. Roll out a sheet at least 8 inches long of each of the color mixes: navy, dark blue, medium blue, and light blue.

3. Roll out three sheets of black clay, each as thin as possible and at least 8 inches long. Set aside one of the sheets to use for wrapping the cane later.

4. Use the blade to cut each of the blue sheets in half crosswise to produce 4-inch lengths. Stack each set of two sheets together and set them on the thin black sheets. Trim the black clay to match (photo 1).

5. Mix the red for the center and roll out a 1 x 8-inch strip. Cut the clay in half crosswise and stack it. Cut out a single square strip 4 inches long and slightly under ¼ inch square (photo 2). Make this piece as square as possible, measuring both sides against the stack, since the entire cane wraps around it.

6. In the following order, lay out the pieces with the black side up: light blue, dark blue, medium blue, and navy. The cane is built by continuously adding two strips of each of these colors to the red center.

7. Begin by placing the red strip on the back of the first color (light blue). Cut the blue clay to the same size as the red strip. Lightly press the strips together. Rotate the cane one turn and place it back on the same color, again facing the black. Cut it to size. Lightly press the clay together (photo 3).

8. Rotate the cane one turn and place it on the next color (dark blue). Cut it to size. Rotate it one turn and place it back on the same color and cut it to size. Repeat this rotation, cutting the pieces to size as you work through all of the colors twice (photo 4).

9. Use the reserve sheet of black clay to wrap around the cane. To do this, wrap each side before cutting it to size. Keep the corners sharper by cutting each side.

10. Reduce the cane to about ½ inch square (or about 36 inches long). Do this by first placing it between the heels of your hands and pressing it. Rotate it and then do it again and again to get the cane to "move." Then press down on it with the heel of your hand, slightly pulling it from one end. When it is finally moving well, pull, twist, and smooth it. At the very end of the reduction, you can use an acrylic brayer to sharpen the corners a bit. Keep in mind that you will distort the cane if you don't do this carefully.

11. Trim the scrap from the ends. Cut the cane into nine equal segments (photo 5). Firmly place these pieces together in three rows of three cane segments, carefully matching the corners (photo 6). Place the three rows together, forming a second cane, and reduce it to approximately 1-inch square (photo 7 on page 70). Cut this cane into four equal pieces.

(continued on page 70)

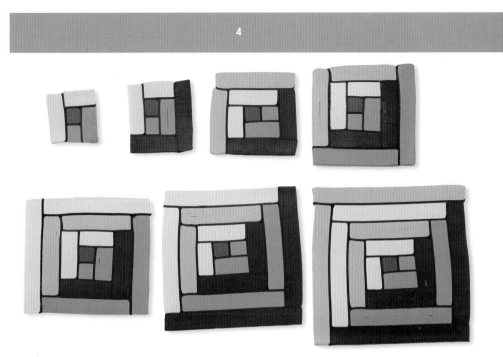

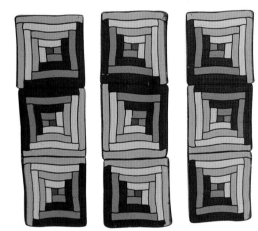

12. You can form several interesting patterns with these four cane segments. When you assemble the canes, make two rows of two segments. Then place the rows together again, carefully matching the corners (photo 8).

13. Reduce the cane to a size of your choice for your pin. (If you want to make matching earrings, you can reduce part of the cane to a smaller size.) For wrapping the cane, roll out a thick sheet of clay from one of the original colors. If you wrap the cane with a solid sheet, the corners will be rounded. Or cut the wrap color to fit the cane sides, and smooth out the seam line with your finger to create square corners.

14. Cut thin slices from the finished cane to make pins or earrings. You can allow them to stay flat or drape them. To smooth the edges on a flat piece, place it between two sheets of thin plastic and smooth the edges through the plastic to remove fingerprints, leaving a smooth surface.

15. To make a draped form that looks like a piece of cloth being held by its corner, place the cane slice between the two sheets of plastic and make the folds with the plastic in place. Fold the center first before folding towards one corner to make each of the outside folds. Carefully remove the plastic. You might want to practice this with solid clay a couple of times!

16. Attach the pin back with a piece of clay (see page 20).

17. Place these pieces facedown on index cards and cure them at 275°F or according to the clay manufacturer's recommendations.

NOTE: See photo 9 for some variations on this pattern made by assembling the four cane segments in different patterns.

Below are some other color possibilities to use for canes, as shown in the photos.

Green quilt (below):

Dark sap green (unmixed)

Medium green= 1 part sap green + 2 parts cadmium yellow

Light green= 1 part sap green + 4 parts cadmium yellow

Lighter green= 1 part light green (mixed above), 1 part ivory (1 part ecru + 1 part white)

Rust quilt (page 67):

Dark rust= 1 part cadmium red + 1 part burnt umber

Light rust= 1 part each of cadmium red, burnt umber, ecru, white

Dark gold= 1 part cadmium yellow + 1 part ecru + $\frac{1}{2}$ part raw sienna or dark ocher

Light gold= 1 part cadmium yellow + 2 parts ecru + 1 part white + $\frac{1}{4}$ part raw sienna or dark ocher

7

8

9

Glass Tile Bracelet

ARTIST

Jennifer Bezingue

T

THE GLASS-LIKE INSETS ON THIS LOVELY BRACELET ARE MADE WITH THE SAME POLYMER TECHNIQUE DESCRIBED IN THE PROJECT ON PAGE 54. THE SHIMMERING SURFACES CHANGE WITH THE LIGHT, EMULATING THE QUALITIES OF GLASS.

MATERIALS

Polymer clay: pearlescent, darker clays, and translucent

Waxed paper

Opaque polyester glitter

Mica powder

Wet/dry sandpaper in range of coarsest to finest grits (220 to 2000)

Cyanoacrylate glue

Sterling silver bezel settings, jump rings, and slide clasp

TOOLS

Pasta machine

Acrylic brayer

Miniature shape cutters

Craft knife

Clay burnishing tool

Baking sheet

Safety glasses

Electric buffing machine with unstitched muslin wheel

2 pairs of chain-nose pliers

PROCESS

1. Mix pearlescent clay and darker clay to the desired color. Roll through the pasta machine at the thickest setting. Cut the sheet in half and stack the layers. Firmly roll the layers together with an acrylic brayer to create the base sheet.

2. Use the pasta machine to roll out a thin sheet of translucent clay. Smooth the sheet onto a layer of waxed paper, and pour small piles of opaque glitter on it. Rub the glitter evenly into the sheet. Shake off any excess glitter and place the sheet on waxed paper, with the glitter side facing up.

3. To create a mica-powder sheet, roll out a ball of the translucent clay that is ½ inch in diameter. Mix in the powder until the clay is stiff, and roll it out on a thin setting.

4. Using miniature shape cutters and craft knife, cut pieces from the glitter sheet and place them glitter-side-down on the base sheet. Next, use the shape cutters and craft knife to cut out shapes from the mica-laden sheet. Place them on the base sheet. Press the appliqués firmly into the bead until they are level with the surface. Cover half to three-quarters of the sheet with both types of appliqués.

5. Cover the appliqués with waxed paper, and burnish them until fully incorporated into the surface, with no seams visible between the translucent and colored clay. Add a second layer of appliqués, pressing them into the surface of the bead, and overlapping them as you wish.

6. Cut squares from the sheet to fit the pre-made sterling silver bezels. Press the squares into bezels and bake for 30 minutes at 275°F. Remove the piece from the oven and immerse it in cold water to improve the clay's translucency.

7. When cool, pry the insets out of bezels with the edge of the craft knife. Tear the various grits of wet/dry sandpaper sheets into quarters. Put one piece of each into warm water for a few minutes until saturated. Begin hand sanding with the coarsest (220 grit) paper. Sand the surface of each inset until it's smooth and the glitter appliqués come into sharp focus. If needed, spot-sand the appliqués that are less clear. When the inset is smooth, continue sanding it with the successive grits of sandpaper (through 2,000 grit).

8. Wearing safety glasses, buff the insets at medium speed until the surface is glass-like.

9. Glue the insets into bezels with cyanoacrylate glue.

10. Use chain-nose pliers to open and close the jump rings to connect the bezels (photo 1). Attach the clasp.

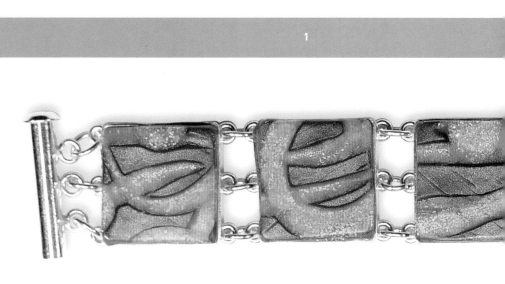

Fresco Beads

ARTIST

SL Savarick

THESE
BEAUTIFULLY
TEXTURED BEADS
IMITATE FRESCO'S
MATTE SURFACE.
POLYMER MAKES
A PERFECT BASE
FOR THE GELATIN
COATING THAT IS
USED TO CREATE
THIS EFFECT.

MATERIALS

Polymer clay: scrap clay, black, gold

Card stock, tile, or other flat surface

Rabbit-skin glue granules (available through art supply stores)

Powdered marble dust/calcium carbonate powder (available through art supply stores)

8 x 10-inch upholstery foam block

Direct dyes or concentrated liquid water-colors in various shades

Plastic wrap

Cyanoacrylate glue

$3/32$-inch Buna rubber cord, 24 inches long

TOOLS

Pasta machine

2-inch circle cutter

Sheet of glass or acrylic, approx. 6 x 6 x $1/4$ inch

Needle tool

Bamboo skewers

Measuring cup and measuring spoons

Glass jar (12 to 14 oz)

Candy thermometer

Small saucepan

Eyedroppers

Cosmetic sponges

Spray bottle with fine mist setting

$1/4$-inch circle punch

Pin vise fitted with $3/32$-inch bit

PROCESS

1. To make the base beads, condition and roll the scrap clay into a sheet that is approximately $1/8$-inch thick. Use the 2-inch circle cutter to cut out 16 circles. Roll two of the clay circles between your palms and form them into balls.

2. Use the glass or acrylic square to slightly flatten both beads at the same time, applying even pressure. Make sure the resulting beads are the same height.

3. Cure both beads for 60 minutes at 275°F and let them cool. These beads will be used as your guides for forming the other beads.

4. Place the cooled guide beads on your work surface with the glass or acrylic on top of them. Roll the remaining 14 circles of clay into balls. Place them between the work surface and sheet to press them until they're the same height as the guides.

5. Use the needle tool to make a shallow indentation in the center of a flattened side on all the beads. Cure the beads for 60 minutes at 275°F on a piece of card stock, tile, or other flat surface.

(continued on page 76)

6. When the beads are fully cured, remove them from the oven and let them cool slightly. While still warm, insert a bamboo skewer into each of the beads, approximately a third of the way in (photo 1). Set the beads aside to cool.

7. To prepare the fresco mixture, use the measuring cup and spoons fill a glass jar with ½ cup of water and sprinkle in 2 level teaspoons of rabbit-skin glue granules. Stir and let the mixture stand for 15 minutes so the granules swell and the mixture resembles applesauce. Add another ½ cup of water and stir until well mixed.

8. Place a candy thermometer in the mixture and put the glass jar in a saucepan. Fill the pan with hot water until it's about halfway up the jar. Place the pan over moderate heat and bring the water to a low simmer.

9. Heat the rabbit-skin glue until the candy thermometer reads 145°F, maintaining this temperature for 15 minutes. Don't allow the temperature to rise above 160°F! Turn the heat down or off as needed to keep the glue heating at the correct temperature. When the time is up, remove the jar from the pan, followed by the thermometer. Add one cup of calcium carbonate powder (powdered marble), and stir the mixture until it's smooth.

10. Replace the candy thermometer and allow the fresco mix to cool to between 100 and 75°F. Use the bamboo skewers as handles to dip the beads one at a time. Dip a bead into the mixture and then hold it over the jar, allowing the excess mixture to drip off. If the mix beads up on the surface the first time you dip it in, simply dip it again and let it drip off. Keep repeating this action until you get a thin coating of fresco mix to cover the surface of the bead (photo 1). Stick the other end of the skewer into the upholstery foam block to dry.

1

11. Use the same process to dip all 14 beads. After applying one coat of fresco, allow each to sit for a few minutes in the upholstery block and dip them again for a second and a final third coat.

12. Allow the beads to sit for approximately 30 minutes.

13. To dye the frescoed beads, place a clean glass or acrylic sheet on your work surface. Use a separate eyedropper to drop six to 10 drops of three to six colors of direct instant-set liquid dyes or one drop of each of your selected colors of concentrated liquid watercolors on the sheet. Add six to 10 drops of water to the dye or watercolor, depending on the color intensity you want.

14. Use a clean cosmetic sponge to apply each color (photo 1). Layer the colors to create subtle color shifts, applying the dye in multiple layers. Set the beads in the foam block to sit for a few minutes, allowing the dye to seep into the bead's fresco surface. If you wish, use the spray bottle filled with water to lightly mist the beads as you apply the dye layers. Experiment!

15. Allow the beads to dry for two hours and remove them from the skewers by gently twisting the beads as you pull off the skewers. If there's a white spot left when you remove the skewer, touch it up with a bit of dye on a sponge.

16. Allow the beads to dry and set up for at least 24 hours, but it's a good idea to let them sit for a few days before you assemble the necklace.

17. To make the spacers and findings, condition and roll the gold and black clay into sheets approximately $\frac{1}{16}$-inch thick. Place the black sheet on a sheet of card stock and use the circle punch to cut out 15 black circles. Remove the

excess polymer around the circles without displacing the circles.

18. Place the gold polymer sheet on a sheet of card stock and cover the sheet with plastic wrap. Use the circle punch to cut out 30 gold circles through the wrap. Remove the wrap and excess polymer around the circles without moving the circles.

19. Cure the spacers on the card stock for 30 minutes at 275°F. Cool them and remove them from the card stock. Set them aside.

20. Condition the remaining black polymer. Shape a loop and toggle clasp from the black polymer and cure it for an hour at 275°F.

21. To assemble the necklace, use the pin vise to drill a $\frac{1}{32}$-inch hole in each of the 14 beads, following the guide of the previously made indentations.

22. To make the spacers, sandwich a black spacer between two gold ones. The gold spacers will have curved edges created by the plastic wrap, so make sure those edges curve inward toward the black spacers. Glue them together with drops of cyanoacrylate glue. Use a needle tool to mark the center of each spacer, and drill each with a $\frac{3}{32}$-inch hole in the center.

23. Cut a 24-inch length of Buna cord. String the necklace, beginning with a spacer and alternating with fresco beads. Finish the strand with a spacer bead.

24. Make a toggle and loop from polymer clay. Use the $\frac{3}{32}$-inch drill tool to drill a small hole in the toggle and loop, without drilling all the way through it. Size the necklace and glue the findings on the Buna cord with a drop of cyanoacrylate glue.

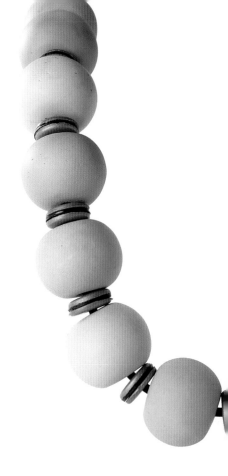

Broken Heart Necklace

ARTIST

Jacqueline Lee

THE PENDANT ON
THIS DELICATE
NECKLACE IS
REVERSIBLE. ONE
SIDE OF THE HEART
IS WHOLE, WHILE
THE OTHER
APPEARS BROKEN.

MATERIALS

Polymer clay: black, orange
  and magenta

Black necklace cord, 1 yard

Cyanoacrylate glue

Waxed paper

Clear liquid polymer medium

Micro-fine polyester glitter: burnt orange
  and fuchsia

8 straight pins with black ball heads

6 mm round black wooden bead

TOOLS

Pasta machine

Flat rubberstamp with patterned surface

Spray bottle

Acrylic roller

Tissue blade

Craft knife with a #11 blade

Pin vise with #74 drill bit and a drill bit
  the diameter of the necklace cord

Wire cutters

Sharp scissors

PROCESS

1. Coat 1 inch of each end of the pendant cord with glue and hang it to dry.

2. Condition the clay. Use the pasta machine to roll out a sheet of black to a medium thickness.

3. Place the rubber stamp, pattern side up, on your work surface. Fill the spray bottle with water and heavily spray the surface of the stamp. Lay the sheet of clay on it and cover it with waxed paper. Firmly roll the clay with the acrylic roller.

4. Gently lift the clay from the stamp and lay it on your work surface with the textured side up. Use the craft knife to cut out two clay rectangles from the clay that measure 1 x 1¾ inches each. Use the tissue blade to trim the outside edges. Cut out an interior rectangle from each piece, creating ¼-inch frames (photo 1, page 80). Bake these pieces at 275°F for 15 minutes or according to the clay manufacturer's suggestions.

5. Make a Skinner Blend from orange and magenta clay on the thickest setting of your pasta machine (photo 2, page 80).

6. Score the back of one of the baked frames and apply a very thin coat of liquid medium. Press it onto the blended clay. Trim the outside edges of the clay to within ¹⁄₁₆ inch of the frame. Trim the inside clay flush with the interior edges.

7. Score the back of the second frame and apply a thin coat of liquid medium. Turn over the frame piece and press the second frame into place on the blended clay layer so the frame appears the same from either side (photo 3, page 80).

(continued on page 80)

1   2   3

8. Roll two 5mm balls and one 6mm ball of black clay. Flatten one of the 5mm balls into a roundel shape and press it onto the top raw edge of the frame in the center, as shown on the finished piece. Press the 6mm ball onto the roundel to form the top piece. Apply a small amount of liquid medium between them to ensure a strong bond.

9. Adhere the other 5mm ball onto the center of the bottom edge of the frame with a bit of liquid medium.

10. Shape a small heart from black clay to fit inside the frame. Embellish the heart with glitter. Use the craft knife to cut a jagged tear across the heart on one side. Bake the frame and the heart at 275°F for an hour and allow the pieces to cool.

11. Using the pin vise fitted with a #74 drill bit, drill four equidistant holes down the left and right sides (through the middle layer) of the frame.

12. Use a drill bit the diameter of your necklace cord to drill a horizontal hole through the 6mm ball on top of the frame.

13. Hold the heart in the center of the frame and insert pins in each of the second holes from the top of the frame. Pierce the heart slightly and mark it. Take the heart out of the frame. Use the #74 drill bit to drill a hole through the center of it at the marked points.

14. Place the heart back inside the frame, and insert the pins into the heart.

15. Use wire cutters to trim two pins to ¼ inch each. Insert the pins into the holes located in the third position from the top. Trim the remaining four pins to about ½ inch and insert them in the top and bottom holes in the frame.

16. Use sharp scissors to trim the dry, stiffened ends of the pendant cord to a sharp angle and thread one end through the 6mm ball at the top of the frame. Thread the ends of the cord, one at a time, through the 6mm wooden bead. The cord should fit snugly in the bead so the bead stays in place when the ends of the cord are pulled to adjust the length.

17. Tie knots in the cord ends. Place a tiny dot of glue on the knots to secure them. When the glue is dry, trim the excess cord flush with each knot.

Photo Transfer Pin

ARTIST

Stephanie Jones Rubiano

TRANSFER AN OLD PHOTO TO CLAY TO CREATE A WHIMSICAL PIN. ADD BITS OF COLLAGE AND METAL TO ADD DIMENSION.

MATERIALS

Polymer clay: white

Color copier

Photo or printed image of your choice
  with simple outline and light colors

Gin (for solvent)

Unlined index card

320-grit sandpaper

Colored pencils

Acrylic matte varnish

Acrylic paints, permanent markers,
  decorative papers

PVA glue

Thin gauge metal

Tiny nuts and bolts

Cyanoacrylate glue

TOOLS

Scissors

Pasta machine

Bone folder

Craft knife

Metal shears

Jeweler's metal file

Pin vise with bits

Chain-nose pliers

PROCESS

1. Choose a photo and make a photo-copy of it, reducing it as needed (photo 1). The image will be reversed after you transfer it. Use scissors to cut out the image, leaving no border.

2. Condition the white clay and roll it through the pasta machine to create a sheet that is ³⁄₁₆ to ⅛-inch thick. Place the image facedown on the clay and burnish it with your fingertip for one minute. Burnish it again with the bone folder, making certain all edges of the image make contact with the clay (photo 2).

3. With the craft knife blade perpendicular to the cutting surface, cut around the edge of the image. Burnish the edges back down with a bone folder. Wet the image with gin and burnish it lightly with a bone folder. Use just enough gin to dampen the paper. After burnishing, you should be able to see the image through the paper (photo 3).

1   2   3

4   5   6

4. Gently roll the paper off, working towards the edges to prevent the image from lifting off the clay. Rewet the paper as necessary to help remove the paper (photo 4). Don't oversaturate the paper, or you'll smear the ink as you rub off the paper.

5. Clean the edges of the piece and place it on an index card. Cure it for 15 minutes at 275°F or according to the manufacturer's instructions. After curing, sand the edges with 320-grit sandpaper (photo 5). Correct any flaws in the image color with colored pencils. Apply a thin coat of acrylic matte varnish and allow it to dry thoroughly.

6. Decorate the piece using acrylic paint, permanent marking pens, and collaged paper adhered with PVA glue. Allow everything to dry before applying another thin coat of acrylic matte varnish (photo 6).

7. Use the metal shears to cut out decorative pieces from thin gauged metal, such as the wings shown in the project photo on page 81. Use the jeweler's file to file away any sharp edges. Use a pin vise to drill holes in the pieces for attaching them to the pin.

8. Drill corresponding holes in the piece and attach the decorative elements with the tiny nuts and bolts. Use chain-nose pliers to tighten the nuts. Apply a small dab of cyanoacrylate glue to the back of the bolts.

Delicate Flower Brooch

ARTIST

Sandra McCaw

INSPIRED BY THE
ARTIST'S LOVE OF
GARDENING, THIS
BROOCH IS MADE
USING TWO FAIRLY
COMPLEX CANES.
YOU CAN ALSO USE
SIMPLE CANES WITH
PLEASING COLOR
COMBINATIONS AND
GRADUATED SHADES.

MATERIALS

Polymer clay: two mixed colors and white for creating shade variations

Decorative bead (optional)

Pin back

TOOLS

Pasta machine

Tissue blade

Acrylic roller

Deli wrap

Dentist's spatula tool (available through dental supplier)

PROCESS FOR CANES

1. Once you've decided on and mixed the two basic colors, begin by mixing 10 progressive shades of each of the two colors. Once this is accomplished, you can begin to build the canes.

2. To build canes 1½ inch square by 2 inches long, begin by cutting a paper template of this size. Use a pasta machine to roll out sheets of clay approximately ³⁄₁₆ inch thick. Make two stacks, one of each color, beginning with a single layer of the lightest shade and two layers of each progressive shade, ending with one layer of the darkest shade. As you stack, use the paper template to cut each sheet to the correct size. Slices from these canes are used to create the intricate patterning of the petals (photo 1).

3. The design used for this project is a saw tooth pattern. The idea is to cut through the length of each cane with your blade in exactly the same pattern, interchanging each piece as it's cut. It's important to work slowly and precisely when cutting through the canes. The more precision employed at this stage, the more successful the completed canes will be.

4. Begin the saw tooth design as shown in photo 2, below. Complete the design as shown in photo 3 on page 86. Make a diagonal cut through the middle of each cane, interchanging each half and flipping it over so the lines meet at right angles (photo 4, page 86).

(continued on page 86)

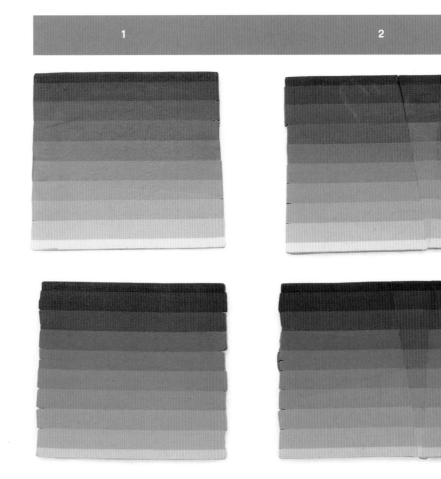

5. Reduce each cane by standing it on end and pressing repeatedly towards the center from opposite sides. Turn it 90° and press again. Flip the cane over and continue pressing. Once the cane is too long to continue in this manner, lay it on the work surface and slide the roller along the length, pulling gently at one end. Rotate it to work on all sides. Reduce it to about ⅝ inch wide to create a cane for a brooch similar to the one shown here, which is 2 inches in diameter.

6. Follow this procedure to make two or three square canes.

PROCESS FOR THE BROOCH

1. To make the petal shapes, press one corner of the square cane toward the center and make it curved. Flatten the opposite corner, leaving two pointed ends that simulate a petal or pinwheel shape. Form the other petal-shaped canes the same way.

2. Use the tissue blade to cut several thin slices from each cane. Play around with them a bit to decide which ones you want to use for each layer of the flower. Keep in mind that you can use the canes slices in different orders or flip them around to get various results. Once that design decision is made, proceed with the construction.

3. Cut 11 or 12 very thin slices to be used for the center layer of petals. Place them on top of a piece of deli wrap so you can move the paper around as you place the petals. Lift each petal with the dental tool as you arrange them in a circle, overlapping them in the center, as shown (photo 5).

4. When the circle is complete, use the dental tool to lift up the first petal from the center and overlap the top of the last petal set in place (photo 6). Press them lightly so they adhere to one another, taking care to not distort the petals.

5. Cut the same number of slices from the second cane layer and place them in a circle around the edges of the paper so they're easier to access. Lift up

3

4

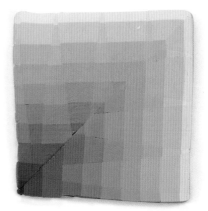

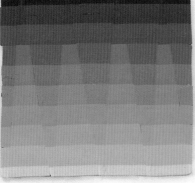

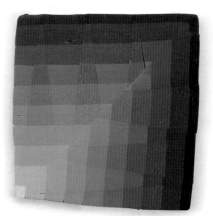

5	**6**	**7**

the first layer of petals as one unit and place it on top of each individual petal to form the second layer (photo 7). Continue in this manner until the second layer is complete.

6. Repeat step 5 to add a third layer of petals (photo 8).

7. Roll out a sheet of very thin clay (about ⅟₁₆ inch thick) in a coordinating color to use for the backing. Lift the entire piece and place it on the sheet of clay. Press gently to secure it to the backing. Use a tissue blade to cut away the excess clay (photo 9).

8. Add a dot of clay or a decorative bead to the center of the flower.

9. Bake the pin at 365°F for half an hour or according to the manufacturer's instructions.

10. Add a pin back to the piece as the final step (see page 20).

8	**9**

Mosaic House Brooch

ARTIST

Lindly Haunani

USE A CLEVER METHOD TO CREATE A CLAY MOSAIC BROOCH. SIMPLY PLACE STRIPS OF COLORFUL BLENDED CLAY ON A BASE BEFORE IMPRESSING THEM WITH GROUT LINES.

MATERIALS

Polymer clay: cool yellow/zinc, warm yellow/cadmium, cool red/fuchsia, warm red/cadmium, cool blue/ultramarine, warm blue/cobalt, white, walnut-sized piece of well-conditioned clay for grout, well-conditioned dark clay for the base

Paper towels

Isopropyl alcohol

Cotton swabs

600-grit wet/dry sandpaper (optional)

Pin back

TOOLS

Pasta machine

Tissue blade

T-pin, hatpin, or wire paper clip

1 x 2-inch piece of stiff plastic cut from an old credit card or other source

PROCESS

1. Begin by mixing the two yellow clays together. Fold the clay and run it through your pasta machine on the thickest setting until you end up with a piece of clay that is 2 inches wide.

2. Mix the two reds together. Fold and run them through the machine on the thickest setting until the piece is 1½ inches wide. Repeat this process with the two blues.

3. Use these colors to make a Skinner Blend (photo 1). Fold the blend in the same direction, running it through your pasta machine 20 to 30 times, or until the colors are nicely blended. The clay will blend more quickly if you carefully align the outer edges when you fold them each time. Make the last pass through the machine at a medium setting.

4. Thoroughly condition the dark clay for the base before rolling out a sheet on your pasta machine at a medium setting. Use the tissue blade to cut a rectangle from the clay for the house shape.

(continued on page 90)

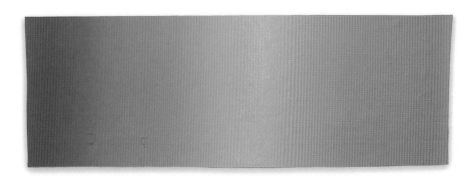

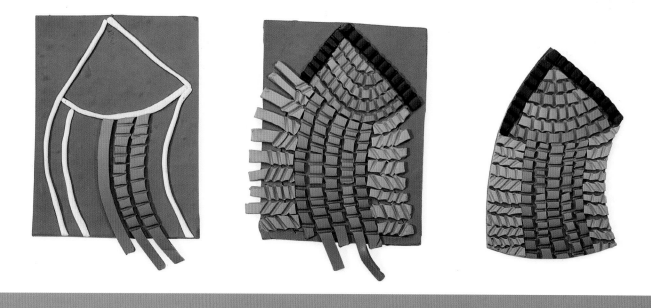

| 2 | 3 | 4 |

5. Outline the house shape by drawing it in the clay or use narrow snakes of clay to define the borders. Cut ¼-inch strips from the Skinner Blend and begin by laying one in the center of your design. Add more strips and use the blunt end of T-pin, hatpin, or wire paper clip to impress grout lines (photo 2).

6. Continue adding strips to fill in the center of the piece, curving them slightly to conform to the shape. Leave space for a border around them and add horizontal strips (photo 3). Fill in the roof with strips.

7. After all of the tiles have been laid, use a tissue blade to trim the edges of the brooch (photo 4). Cure the piece at 275°F for 40 minutes or according to the clay manufacturer's instructions. Allow it to cool to room temperature.

8. To add grout to the piece, use thoroughly warmed and conditioned clay. Keep in mind that the grout color you choose affects the overall look of the piece. (Instead of using white, try mixing all of the warm and cool primaries together to make a warm tan color. Or use a dark grey instead of black.)

9. Use the piece of plastic to firmly press grout into a small area of the piece, moving in more than one direction (photo 5). Remove as much clay as you can from the surface, while being careful not to pull off tiles that haven't yet been grouted. Grout the whole piece (photo 6). Use a paper towel saturated with alcohol to clean the excess grout from the tiles. If small detailed areas need further cleanup, use a cotton swab moistened with alcohol.

10. Cure the piece according to the clay manufacturer's directions. Allow the piece to cool to room temperature. Sand away small amounts of excess grout with wet/dry 600-grit sandpaper, keeping in mind that part of the charm and authenticity of the mosaic is an imperfect surface.

11. Attach the pin back with polymer clay (see page 20).

| 5 | 6 |

Sculptural Pod Necklace

ARTIST

Jeffrey Lloyd Dever

NATURE INFORMS THE AESTHETICS OF THIS EXQUISITE NECKPIECE. ALTHOUGH IT IS CHALLENGING, MAKING A HOLLOW FORM CAN BE ACCOMPLISHED WITH PATIENCE AND PRACTICE.

MATERIALS

Polymer clay in various colors
 (contrasting colors suggested)

Heavy cardstock

Cyanoacrylate glue

Toothpick or glue applicator

Dust mask

Sandpaper (100 grit, 220 grit, or higher
 grit for more refinement)

Baby wipes

Automotive finish protector

Polyester fiberfill

Aluminum foil

Steel wool (0000 fine)

Buffing wheel (optional)

Anodized niobium wire cable or other
 cord of your choice

Jewelry closure of your choice

TOOLS

Scissors

Craft knife with #11 blade

Metal ruler

Pasta machine

Fine needle tool

Older tissue blade with slightly
 dull edges

Thin-gauge palette knife (optional)

#15 beading needle

Ceramic tile or other hard baking surface

Soft toothbrush

PROCESS FOR FIVE-SIDED POD

1. On the cardstock, draw three identical silhouettes of a symmetrical pod slightly smaller than the finished piece you envision.

2. Use the scissors to cut out two of the shapes. Use the craft knife and ruler to score the two pieces lengthwise down the middle by lightly cutting halfway through the cardstock. Fold these pieces along the score lines.

3. Draw a line down the middle of the third shape, and cut out half of it. You've now created three cardstock pieces to assemble into a five-ribbed structure.

4. In a well-ventilated area, carefully glue together the spines of the first two pieces with a small amount of cyano-acrylate glue, spacing them to allow for the final fifth piece. Hold the piece away from you as you work. If you wish, apply the glue using a toothpick or glue applicator. Avoid getting glue on your skin, since you may bond your fingers together or to the piece.

5. Position the fifth rib along the spine, and glue it in place. When dry, carefully coat all the edges with glue to create a rigid structure (photo 1).

6. Once the structure is dry, fill in each area between the cardstock ribs with scrap clay (photo 2), paying careful attention to the shape you create as you smooth the clay. Don't overfill it. Cure the form at approximately 275°F for 25 to 30 minutes or according to the clay manufacturer's specifications.

7. When the form is cool, put on a dust mask and sand it with 100-grit sandpaper, refining the shape and smoothing the surface.

8. Create a sheet of conditioned scrap clay at the widest setting on the pasta machine. Layer the form one side at a time, trimming it to fit the shape as you go. Pinch the seams together to main-tain the ridges. Smooth it with a moist finger or baby wipe.

9. Use the needle tool to pierce the clay with fine, closely spaced vent holes that allow any trapped air that escape during curing. Cure the piece at 275°F for 25 to 30 minutes or as suggested by the clay manufacturer. When the piece has cooled, sand it to create a pleasing shape, maintaining the ribs with sharp smooth ridges (photo 3).

10. Coat the form with two to three coats of automotive finish protector, which serves as a release agent. Allow each coat to dry. The piece you've creat-ed will serve as an interior form for molding the final pod.

11. Roll out a sheet of clay to serve as your base color at the thickest setting. Cover the mold layer one side at a time, trimming it to fit, and pinch the clay at the joints to maintain distinct ribs.

1

12. Use the tissue blade to carefully slice down opposite sides of the form and then lightly press them together at the seams. Use the fine needle tool to create small vent holes (photo 4). Place the piece on polyester fiberfill to prevent distortion, and cure it at the same temperature and time as before.

13. While the pod is still warm from curing, use a tissue blade or thin-gauge palette knife to gently pry off the exterior pods (photo 5). Remove the interior form. If the clay is too cool and rigid, simply reheat it. Place the halves back together and let them cool completely.

14. Carefully glue the halves together, one side at a time. Be careful not to glue the pod to yourself! Use a fresh baby wipe to blot the excess glue. When the glue is completely dry, sand it with 100-grit sandpaper to refine the shape and smooth the surface. Create sharp ridges on ribs and pointed ends by sanding toward the edge as if you're sharpening a knife. Use a fresh baby wipe to clean the pod thoroughly, removing all dust and residue (photo 6).

15. Roll out thin sheets of clay for the final layer. You can use contrasting colors for various sides, if you wish. It's nice to use a Skinner Blend in a value that contrasts with the pod's base color, since that underlying color will be revealed when you sand the ridges.

16. Apply clay to one of the sides of the pod, paying special attention to working the air bubbles out by gently pressing from the center of the layer to the edges along the ribs. Use the older tissue blade or thin-gauge palette knife to carefully trim the layer from tip to tip along the rib. (A sharp blade might cut into the form's ribs.) Smooth the edges, leaving just a bit of the underlying color exposed along the rib. You might need to repeat this step several times until the clay is thin and smooth enough at the rib edges.

17. Create an ultra-fine needle tool by forming a handle from polymer clay and embedding a #15 beading needle in it. Cure the piece. Use the tool to repeatedly pierce this layer with fine, closely spaced vent holes. With a moist clean finger, gently stroke the clay's surface repeatedly until the vent holes disappear. Doing this allows trapped air to be ventilated during curing, while giving the surface an appearance of perfect smoothness.

18. Now that you've applied clay to one side only, cure the piece at the same temperature and amount of time as before. Curing each side separately will allow you to work with the piece without damaging the raw clay. Sand, smooth, and polish the piece after you apply and cure the sides, beginning with 220-grit and finishing with 0000 steel wool. If you want a more polished look, finish with a higher grit sandpaper and buffing wheel.

(continued on page 94)

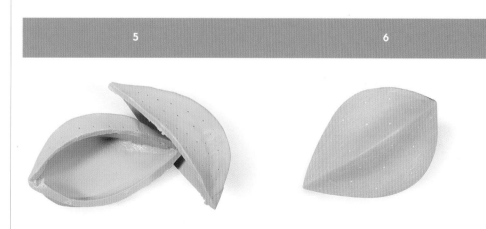

PROCESS FOR LONG POD

1. Create a slender, pointed form out of scrap clay by rolling a snake slightly smaller in length and diameter than the finished pod. Cure it at 275°F for 25 to 30 minutes or according to the clay manufacturer's instructions. When cool, put on a dust mask and sand it with 100-grit sandpaper to smooth and refine the shape. Finish the form with pointed ends (photo 7).

2. As you did for the five-sided pod, coat the form with two to three coats of automotive finish protector to act as a release agent, allowing each coat to dry. Roll out a thick layer of conditioned clay to serve as your base color. Layer the form with the sheet of clay, gently coaxing the sheet to conform to the pod without wrinkles. Slice an edge of the sheet along the length of the pod and wrap the other edge around it, trimming it to abut the first edge. Press them together firmly and smooth the seam, being careful to maintain the shape without deforming the surface.

3. Slice carefully down opposite sides of the form. Then lightly press them together so the form can be removed later. Use a fine needle tool to create small vent holes on the entire surface (photo 8). Place the form on polyester fiberfill and cure it at the same

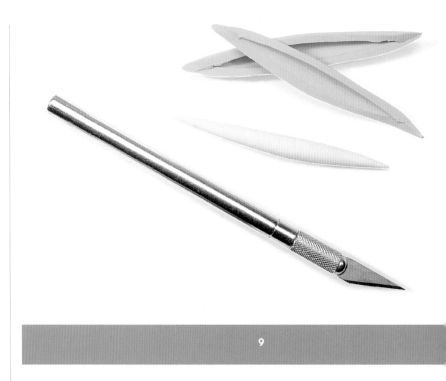

9

temperature and time as before.

4. While the clay is still warm and pliable, use a tissue blade or thin-gauge palette knife to gently pry the pod halves from the form (photo 9). If the clay is too cool and rigid, simply reheat and repeat. Place the halves together and let them cool.

5. Carefully glue the halves together one side at a time with cyanoacrylate glue, blotting with a baby wipe as needed. When completely dry, sand the shape with 100-grit sandpaper to refine it and smooth the surface. Clean it thoroughly and remove all dust or residue with a fresh baby wipe (photo 10).

6. Roll out a thin finishing layer, such as a Skinner Blend, in a value that contrasts with the underlying pod.

7. Draw a guideline for your clay seam along the length of the backside. Apply the clay by slightly overlapping the guideline before gently coaxing the sheet around the pod. Take care to avoid wrinkles or trapped air bubbles. Slice the starting edge of the sheet along the guideline and wrap the opposing edge around, trimming it to abut the first edge. Press them together very gently, smoothing and closing the

7

8

seam as you go. Be careful to leave the surface as smooth as possible because this thin layer does not leave much material to be sanded away later.

8. Use the #15 beading needle tool (created for the five-sided pod in step 17) to repeatedly pierce this layer with fine, closely spaced vent holes. With a moist clean finger, gently stroke the clay surface until the vent holes disappear. Cure at the same temperature and time as before.

9. When the piece has cooled, sand, smooth, and polish it, starting with 220-grit sandpaper and finishing with 0000 steel wool (photo 11). If you want a more polished look, finish with higher grit sandpaper and a buffing wheel.

10. Use a craft knife fitted with a #11 blade to create the randomly spaced, conical-shaped holes on the pod's surface that reveal interior color (photo 12).

To do this, gently place the point of a sharp blade perpendicular to the pod's surface. Under light pressure, smoothly rotate the knife as if you're twisting a pencil in your hand. (It's simple but might take a little practice.) Vary the number of rotations to change the size of the hole. Consistently keep the pressure light.

11. When finished, blow out all the shavings and clean the holes with the soft toothbrush.

12. To assemble the necklace, drill holes in the pods with a bit the size of your cable or cord. Soften the edges by sanding them with a small wad of steel wool, reaching into each hole as you do this.

13. String the pods onto the cable or cord and finish with a closure of your choice. The pods can be worn spaced apart or close together.

12

Millefiore Pendants and Pins

ARTIST

Lindly Haunani

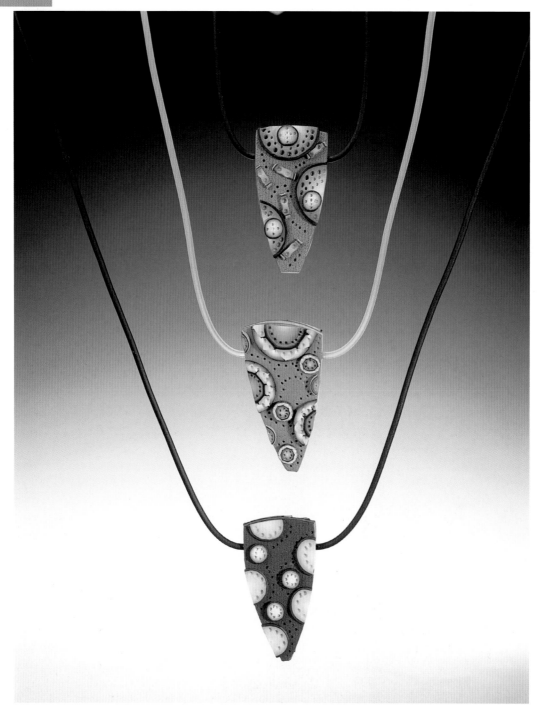

INSPIRED IN PART BY PATTERNED FABRIC, SLICES OF SIMPLE MILLEFIORE CANE ARE USED AS GRAPHIC ELEMENTS TO ENHANCE VIBRANT PENDANTS AND PINS.

MATERIALS

Polymer clay: cadmium yellow, fuchsia, ultramarine, white, black

Waxed paper

36-grit sandpaper

Pin backs

28 inches of rubber or plastic cording

Cyanoacrylate glue

TOOLS

Pasta machine

Tissue blade

Ball burnisher

Acrylic roller/brayer

Pin vise and bit corresponding to diameter of your cording

PROCESS

1. You'll need at least three different clay colors to make the simplest decorative cane that serves as the center of a more complex cane, or is used alone as a decorative dot. Some examples of the particular color mixes used in this project include the following:

Deep navy blue= 1 part ultramarine + 3 parts black

Vibrant purple= 2 parts ultramarine + one part fuchsia + pea-sized bit of white

Deep olive= 2 parts cadmium yellow + 2 parts ultramarine

Yellow green= 7 parts cadmium yellow + 1 part ultramarine

Creme yellow= 17 parts white + 1 part cadmium yellow

Red-orange= 7 parts cadmium yellow + 1 part fuchsia

2. Create a Skinner Blend for the cane's center from a lighter and darker valued color, such as vibrant purple and white or red orange and creme yellow. When you make the final pass of the clay through the pasta machine, roll it at the thickest setting. The resultant piece will be about 6 inches wide.

3. Fold the clay in thirds lengthwise (maintaining the orientation of the clay from light to dark). It will be about 2 inches wide and the same length. Put the narrow end of the clay through at the thickest setting and roll it, followed by another roll on the medium setting. By doing this, you'll create a length of clay with very gradual color shifts (photo 1). When you roll up the clay to make a cane, there won't be choppy breaks in the color.

(continued on page 98)

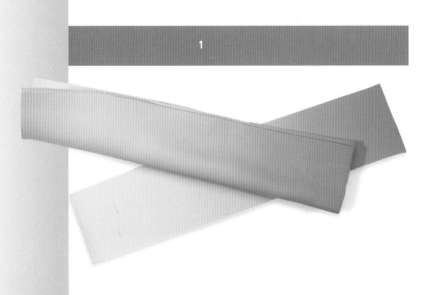

1

4. The thin piece of clay will be about 18 inches long and somewhat difficult to handle. Therefore, lay it out on a piece of waxed paper before you try to maneuver it. At the lighter-colored end, use the tissue blade to trim it crosswise, creating a straight edge and eliminating about 1/8 inch of clay. Roll the trimmed piece into a smooth and even snake. Lay it along the cut edge and smooth it into the edge. Use this small "rolling pin" to slowly and carefully roll up the strip of clay (photo 2). Avoid making air pockets. Blend the cut edge by smoothing and smudging the edge into the roll. On a flat surface, roll and reduce it slightly, taking care to make a round cylinder.

5. To make the cane's outer wrap, roll out a darker-valued clay on the middle setting of your pasta machine. Trim one end of the clay, tack it onto your cane, and roll the cane a bit farther than a complete wrap, making an impression with the edge. Unroll the cane and cut your seam line along this line. On a flat surface, gently roll it with your hand through the entire circumference to reduce it slightly and consolidate the clay.

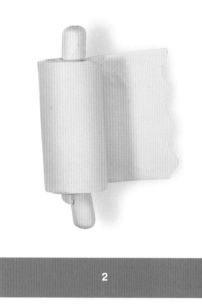

2

6. Slice off a 1-inch section from your cane and reduce it until it is about ⅛ inch in diameter. Slices of this dot cane can be used as tiny accents in your design between or on top of slices of larger cane.

7. To make a more complex cane, add one or more bands of color to this small cane, each followed by a darker wrap. (Follow the steps already outlined to do this.) When you've finished adding layers, reduce this cane to a diameter of about 1 inch or less (photo 3). Allow the cane to rest before cutting it into 1⁄16-inch slices.

8. Next, prepare the base clay for your pendant or pin. It's nice to add an interior layer of contrasting color between two darker colors to create a contrasting line along the edge of the pendant or pin. To do this, sheet the base clay at the thickest setting on your pasta machine. Roll out a medium-thickness sheet of con-trasting color and lay it on top of the first sheet. Run it through the machine on the thickest setting. Fold the resulting piece in half, toward the interior color, and use the ball burnisher to lightly burnish it to remove any air bubbles. Lay the 36-grit sandpaper on your base sheet and gently burnish the back of it to create texture. Use the flexible tissue blade to cut out a shape of your choice from a piece of heavy paper.

9. Next, decorate your pendant or pin with cane slices, allowing some of them to overlap the edges (photo 4). Use the acrylic roller/brayer to gently adhere them before turning the piece over to trim away the excess clay, following the edges of the pendant. Turn the piece back over and add small cane slices as accents. If you wish, slice pieces of cane to create rectangular segments, and use them as decorative elements.

10. Once all elements are in place, turn the pendant right side up. Use the end of the ball burnisher to impress a dot pattern on the decorative elements and the top of the base (photo 5).

11. If you want to decorate the back of the piece, turn it over and add more cane slices. If you are making a pin, attach the pin back with a small piece of clay (see page 20). When you're done, bake the clay for about 30 minutes at about 275°F or according to the clay manufacturer's instructions.

12. To add a cord to a pendant, cut it to a length of your choice. Use the pin vise fitted with a bit that corresponds to the diameter of your cording to drill two ¼-inch-deep holes on opposite sides of your pendants. Secure the ends of the cording inside the hole(s) with a small bit of cyanoacrylate glue.

| 3 | 4 | 5 |

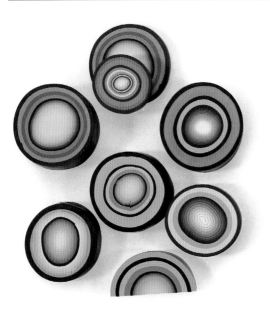

Twists and Turns Necklace

ARTIST

Lindly Haunani

THIS NECKLACE FEATURES ONE OF THE ARTIST'S FAVORITE POLYMER JEWELRY FORMS — TWISTED TUBE BEADS. CLUSTERS OF SCULPTURAL JOINT BEADS DECORATED WITH WILD AND COLORFUL DOTS IN CONTRASTING COLORS LINK THESE WAVY BEADS.

MATERIALS

Polymer clay: medium to dark value color, lightly tinted white or other very light color, black mixed with dark color of your choice, and coordinating colors of your choice

Stiff beading thread, 1 yard

Cyanoacrylate glue

TOOLS

Pasta machine

Tissue blade

Metal knitting needles (01 for tube beads and 000 for joint beads)

Baking pan

PROCESS

1. Make a Skinner Blend from half medium to dark colored clay and a lighter valued color. Follow steps 1 through 6 on pages 97 to 99 to make simple canes that can be sliced into dots. Use the blend for the center of the bulls-eye cane and the mixed black clay for the cane wrap (photo 1).

2. To make the long tube beads, begin with an absolutely straight 01 knitting needle to use as your mandrel. Firmly roll some colored clay of your choice into a round bead to eliminate any air bubbles.

3. Roll the clay into a barrel shape, and mount and center it on the needle. To evenly elongate the clay, roll through the whole circumference of the shape while exerting gentle pressure, moving the clay towards the end of the needle.

(continued on page 102)

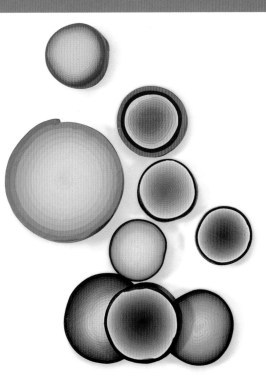

1

4. When the clay is the desired thickness, trim the ends by placing the tissue blade perpendicular to the needle at each end, rolling the bead on the mandrel to cut around the whole bead. Gently remove the clay from the rod and twist it into a slightly curved shape (photo 2).

5. To make the conical beads, roll a small amount of clay into a cylindrical log about ½ inch in diameter and 7 inches long. Cut this log into 14½-inch segments. Use firm pressure to roll

each piece into a round ball, eliminating air pockets and smoothing the bead's surface.

6. Roll the ball into a cone shape by rolling one end to make it narrow. Continue to roll so the form fans out into a cone shape. If you wish, trim the narrow end of the bead. Repeat this process to make as many beads as you like. Pierce the beads through the diameter with narrow knitting needles. Leave the needles intact for curing the beads on a baking pan.

7. To make a variation of this bead form, roll each round bead into a cylindrical log, followed by rolling the center of the log with your forefinger to form a barbell shape (photo 3).

8. Grasp the two ends of the bead and twist it once, forming a shape that has a hole large enough to accommodate the beading thread. Cover the ends of your joint beads with relatively thick ⅛-inch cane slices from your dot cane, adding dimension and texture (photo 3).

9. Cure the beads at 275°F for 45 minutes or according to the clay manufacturer's directions.

10. String the beads onto the beading thread, placing joint beads between tube beads in a design of your choice. Tie off the ends of the wire with a square knot close to the beads. Apply a dot of glue to the knot and let it dry to secure the knot.

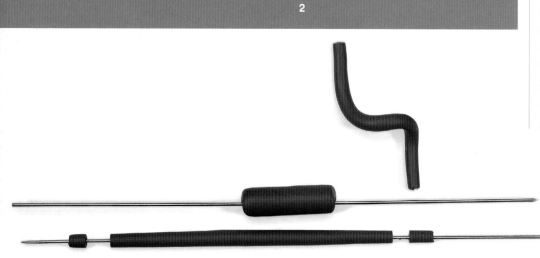

2

3

Flock of Blackbirds Necklace

ARTIST

Leslie Blackford

This artist's love of nature led her to create this unusual necklace made of bird-shaped beads and rustic twigs. The birds are easy to sculpt and the twigs are made with a very simple clay mold.

MATERIALS

Polymer clay: black, brown, scrap clay in any color, small amount of white

Tiny black seed beads

Toothpick

Patina paint

Cyanoacrylate glue

Buna rubber cord or beading wire

Jump ring

Lime-green crystals and cherry quartz beads

Jewelry clasp

TOOLS

Several needle tools or other thin piercing tools

Pin vise with bits

Several sticks or twigs, each about 2 to 3 inches long

Pasta machine

Spray bottle with fine mist setting

Craft knife

PROCESS

1. To begin making the smaller blackbird beads shown on the necklace, select a marble-sized piece of conditioned black clay. Roll the clay into a smooth ball about ½ inch in diameter (photo 1). Place your index finger on half of the ball, and gently roll it a few times against your work surface to create a pear shape. The smaller end of this will be the bird's head (photo 2).

2. Gently pinch the larger end of the pear shape (photo 3). Shape it into a slightly flattened point to create a tail.

3. To add the eyes to the head, use a needle tool to make a shallow indentation for holding a seed bead. Place the bead on the end of the tool and insert it sideways into the indentation, so the hole isn't visible (photo 4).

4. To make the beak, mix a bit of brown or black with white. Shape the clay into a tiny pyramid-shaped form. Place one side of the pyramid slightly below the center of the eyes, and use enough pressure to adhere it to the face. Use the needle tool to lightly carve a thin line to create the appearance of an upper and lower beak (photo 5).

5. Insert a toothpick in the underbelly of the bird and stick the other end of it in the block of scrap clay so you can carve both sides of the bead without distorting it. Use the needle tool or a straight pin to make very light carving strokes on the body, creating a feather-like texture. Begin at the head and move to the tail, following the diagonal shape until you're satisfied with the texture (photo 6).

6. Repeat this process to make four more birds, or as many as you wish for your necklace. If you plan to add a pendant at the bottom, create two birds that are slightly larger, following the same procedure.

7. To cure the beads, place them upright on toothpicks stuck into a scrap block of clay. Bake the beads for one hour at 280°F or according to the clay manufacturer's instructions.

8. After the beads have cooled, use the pin vise to drill holes in all of the birds. Drill into the toothpick indentation and up through the back of the neck so the bead will hang nicely on the necklace.

9. To make twig beads, find several small twigs, each about 2 to 3 inches long. Condition some scrap clay and roll out enough to create a slab long and wide enough to hold the twigs. The mold should be twice the thickness of the twigs. Press the sticks firmly into the mold and remove them (photo 7), leaving their impressions. Bake the mold at 280 to 300°F for one hour, or

according to the clay manufacturer's instructions. Let the mold cool completely.

10. Unevenly mix together equal parts of black and brown clay, leaving striated lines in the clay that resemble wood. Roll out logs large enough in diameter to fill up each mold. Cut the logs to the appropriate lengths.

11. Prepare the mold by misting it with water from the spray bottle. Press in each log and remove it. Make the other side of the piece look "twig-like" by carving shallow lines with a needle tool into the surface, simulating bark texture (photo 8).

12. Use needle tools to pierce holes all the way through each twig. As you do this, handle the pieces very gingerly so you don't disturb the natural bark texture imprinted from the mold. Touch up any finger smudges with the needle tool by scratching the surface to resemble rough bark. Leave the twigs on the needle tools and bake them at the same temperature as the mold for an hour, or according to the manufacturer's directions. After curing, remove them from the needle tools, and let them cool.

13. Rub the twigs with patina paint to make them appear more authentic. Wipe away any excess paint and let it dry.

14. To make the pendant, slightly bend one of the short twigs and place it between the two larger birds, as shown in the main photo on page 103. Trim it with a craft knife, if needed. Use the pin vise to enlarge the needle-tool holes to accommodate the twig ends. Bend the twig slightly, and use cyanoacrylate glue to attach it. Then add a dab of glue between the beaks to hold them together. From one of the twig beads, use a craft knife to cut a short bead (about ½ inch long). Thread a short piece of cord or wire through the jump ring and back through this bead (doubled). Trim the ends of the Buna cord or beading wire and glue them into the holes in the heads of the birds.

15. Cut a piece of cord or beading wire that's about 24 inches long. String on the pendant by its jump ring, and then add the various clay beads with glass and crystal beads between them. Add a jewelry clasp to the ends of the necklace.

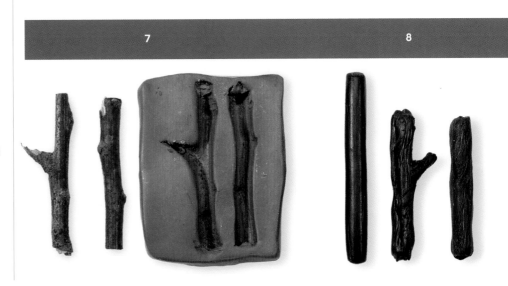

Orbital Bangle Bracelets

ARTIST

Julia Sober

POLYMER CLAY BEADS SERVE TO COVER THE SHARP ENDS OF THE GUITAR STRINGS USED TO MAKE A BRACELET FORM, CREATING A SEAMLESS AND DISTINCTIVE ACCESSORY. UNUSUAL CANES ARE USED TO DECORATE THE SURFACE OF THE BEADS.

MATERIALS

Polymer clay: small amounts of translucent, copper, black, navy, and ecru

Guitar or bass strings, new or used

Cotton batting

600-grit wet/dry sandpaper

Soft cloth

TOOLS

Chain-nose pliers

Wire cutters

Pasta machine

Tissue blade

Needle tool

Large-gauge knitting needle or other wide, round tool

PROCESS

1. Choose a set of three to five (or more) guitar strings for each bracelet, mixing thicker and thinner wires and gold and silver colors. Slightly space apart the ends of the wires with their attached metal discs. Loop the collection of wires and coil the strings around each other several times through the central opening. Leave the last 6 inches or so of each plain wire end free and curl them (photo 1, page 108).

2. Use the chain-nose pliers to secure the sharp ends of any wires by pinching them in three or four places on the form. The beads you add will cover these sharp ends.

3. Begin the bulls-eye cane by rolling a ball of any color polymer clay into a snake, approximately 1 inch thick. Trim it to about 4 inches in length. This piece serves as the middle circle of the cane.

4. To wrap this center snake, roll out a sheet of another color clay at the thickest setting on your pasta machine and cut

one straight edge at the bottom. Trim the sides of this sheet to match the length of your snake. Position the snake horizontally along the bottom edge and roll the sheet around it. Trim the overlap to create a smooth seam. Wrap the cane again in another sheet of clay and trim it.

NOTE: Experiment with various sheet thicknesses to give your canes different looks. Thinner sheets result in fine-lined circles, while thicker sheets add more depth. You can also use a thick sheet of translucent clay as a wrap and define this layer by wrapping it with thin sheets of a light color before adding darker wraps.

5. Reduce the resulting cane by pinching the ends and squeezing towards the center, maintaining pressure around the circumference. This action forces the cane to the center, allowing for faster and more even reduction of the cane. Use your hands to roll the cane against your work surface to lengthen it, maintaining even pressure. Continue reducing and rolling the cane until it is 18 inches long.

6. Use the tissue blade to cut the cane into nine pieces, or another odd number of pieces. Arrange them in a random grouping to create an organic feel (photo 2, page 108). Further reduction will distort the profile of the circles. Once the pieces are arranged to your satisfaction, press them together to adhere the strips and set the cane aside to rest.

7. To create a pointed and oval-shaped variation of this cane, reduce the initial bulls-eye to approximately 16 inches long before pinching down opposite sides along the length of the cane with your thumbs and forefingers. Cut this uneven, bumpy cane into nine pieces. Combine the pieces by overlapping the

(continued on page 108)

pinched ends and wider center parts of different pieces (photo 2, center).

8. To create a cane variation with two lines in the center (photo 2, right) begin with a cylinder of light colored clay approximately 2 inches across and 3 inches long. Set this piece on end to create a short, fat cylinder. To add the black lines, cut through the cylinder from top to bottom with your blade to divide it into three tall pieces.

9. Run a sheet of black clay through a thick setting on your pasta machine. Trim two strips 1 inch wide and 3 inches long from this sheet. Peel the curved sides away from the cut cylinder and place the strips down either side of the rectangular centerpiece. Reassemble the cylinder, trimming the width of the black strips as needed so the lines are completely enclosed within the lighter-colored clay.

10. Squeeze and roll the cylinder against your work surface to round out the sides and wrap it as with contrasting layers of clay as described in step 4. Reduce, cut, and recombine the canes.

Set each grouped cane aside to rest for several minutes. Later, you'll add slices of them to the surface of clay beads.

11. To make simple coiled beads, roll a snake from your desired clay color. Use a sharp blade to cut thin slices from a cane, and apply the slices to the snake. Roll it against your work surface to smooth it. Coil this snake around the bracelet in an open area and press the tapered ends back into the coil to secure the bead.

12. To make rounded beads covered with cane slices, roll a ball of clay in your desired background color before applying slices to the surface. To create depth on the bead's surface, shave extra-thin partial slices from canes containing translucent clay and layer these slices over the others.

13. When a bead is decorated to your satisfaction, roll it lightly between your palms to seal the slices to the surface. When the seams between the slices disappear, shape your bead as desired and set it aside to rest before piercing a hole in it.

14. Use a needle tool to pierce through the bead in a drilling motion, entering from one side of the bead and then the other, keeping the edges of the hole smooth. Widen the holes with a knitting needle or other wider tool to accommodate the bracelet wires and let the bead rest again.

15. To attach the bead to your bracelet, slice it open by running a tissue blade along one side from one hole opening to the other. Pull the cut ends open and fit the cut bead over the bracelet form, keeping the cut side to the center of your bracelet. Press the cut ends back together starting where the bead attaches to the wires and working towards the middle (photo 3). Use your fingers to smooth the seam.

16. When your bracelet is adorned to your liking, tilt it away from your baking surface with batting to keep the beads from flattening during the curing process. Cure the entire bracelet at 275°F for the full baking time. When the piece is cool, sand the outer edges of your beads with 600-grit wet/dry sandpaper. Buff it with a soft cloth to bring out the full depth and translucence in your designs.

1   2   3

Bear Claw Necklace

ARTIST

Leslie Blackford

THE INSPIRATION FOR THIS SCULPTED NECKLACE DERIVED FROM THE ARTIST'S FASCINATION WITH ANCIENT NATIVE AMERICAN CULTURE. SHE DREAMED UP A PIECE THAT MIGHT HAVE ONCE BEEN WORN BY THE PEOPLES OF THIS WORLD.

MATERIALS

Polymer clay: white, beige, translucent, black, bits of red and yellow

Raw umber paint

Two black glass seed beads

Cyanoacrylate glue

Black Buna cord

Accent beads of your choice (trade beads are used here)

TOOLS

Long needle tool

Toothbrush

Pasta machine

Cheese grater

Acrylic rod

Pumice stone

Tissue blade

Patterned rubber stamp

Paintbrush

PROCESS

1. To begin the claw beads, blend together the white and beige clay to make a bone or ivory colored clay. Roll the mixture into a log shape about ¾ inch in diameter and roughly the length of a pencil. Condition the translucent clay and roll it into a log shape of the same size.

2. Place one log on top of the other. Press them firmly together. Roll and squeeze the logs to reduce them without twisting them. As the logs lengthen, cut them in half and stack them again. Firmly press them together again and repeat the reduction process several times until you see very thin lines that run throughout the clay.

3. Roll out a log about ¼ inch in diameter and cut it into equal pieces, each about 2 inches long. Use your fingers and gently roll one end of the piece into a pointed cone. Round off the flat end of the piece. Curve the claw slightly to make it look more authentic (photo 1). Insert a needle tool in the bead near the flat end. Repeat to make 10 to 12 beads for your necklace. Cure the beads at 285°F for about an hour or according to the clay manufacturer's specifications. Let the beads cool off.

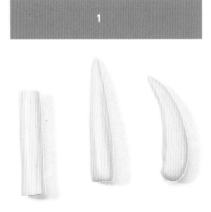

1

2

4. Use the toothbrush to stain the claw beads with raw umber acrylic paint. Wipe away the excess paint.

5. To make the pink coral beads, use the pasta machine to roll out a flat sheet of translucent clay. Use the cheese grater to shred small bits of yellow, red, and beige clay on the clay's surface. Gently roll the acrylic rod over the bits of color, just enough to adhere the tiny pieces. Run the entire sheet through your pasta machine several times until the colors are almost, but not completely, blended together (photo 2).

6. Roll the coral mixture into three logs, each about 3 inches long and about ½ inch in diameter. Use a long needle tool to pierce a hole through the logs. Roll them firmly over the pumice stone to add a rough texture that simulates natural coral. To add more texture, use a needle tool or straight pin to add shallow pinholes to the clay.

7. Cure the logs at 285°F for about an hour, or according to the clay manufacturer's instructions. While they are still very warm, use the tissue blade to cut them into beads. Use the toothbrush to apply raw umber paint to each bead. Wipe away the excess paint and allow it to dry.

8. To create the final piece or pendant, roll out a thin sheet of the coral clay. Press the patterned stamp firmly into the clay and set it aside for the moment.

9. To sculpt the bear's face, start with a ball of black clay resembling a large marble (photo 3). Push the ball against your work surface to flatten the back of it. Pinch the center of the circle to form the snout (photo 4). Using both hands, pinch equal amounts of clay up and outward to begin shaping the ears (photo 5). Continue to round off the shape of them, but be sure to keep them small and close to the head.

10. Use the needle tool to make a shallow indention for the eyes on each side of the head. Put a glass seed bead on the end of the tool and slip it into each indention, making sure that the holes of the seed beads aren't visible (photo 6).

11. To make the nose, roll a very small ball of black clay and smash it so it is flat. Cut it in half and place half of it on the end of the snout to form the nose (photo 7). Round off the edges and use the needle tool to make small indentations beneath it for the nostrils. Use the needle tool to draw lines in the clay on the head to create a fur-like texture. Create indentations in the ears with the end of paintbrush.

12. Place the bear face on the sheet of stamped coral clay. Trim the coral sheet so it frames the bear's head. (If you wish, you can frame the bear's head with half circles of ivory clay placed behind the head, as shown. Create texture in the ivory clay with a needle tool.)

13. Roll out a thin sheet of black clay. Place it underneath the mounted head on coral clay and trim the black clay to ¼ inch larger than the piece, allowing a border around it.

14. Use the tissue blade to cut out a very small slice from the side of one of the coral beads so you can mount it at the top of the bear pendant. Use cyanoacrylate glue to hold it in place.

15. Cut ¼-inch lengths of ivory clay, and cut them into tile-like pieces to apply to the black border. After you're done, trim and round off the edges of the ivory

frame. Cure at 285°F for about one hour, or according to the clay manufacturer's instructions.

16. After the pendant is cool, apply raw umber paint to it with a toothbrush and wipe away the excess. Allow the paint to dry.

17. Cut a 24-inch piece of black Buna cord, and thread the pendant onto it followed by a coral bead on either side. Next, add the black and white accent beads. Continue to add claw and coral beads on either side to complete the necklace.

18. To make the clasp, shown on page 109, form a short bead out of coral clay as well as a short pointed ivory piece. Stick the needle tool through one end of the coral bead for stringing the cord through it later on. Cure the two pieces and let them cool. Remove the needle tool. Drill a shallow hole on the other end of the coral bead in line with the pierced hole. Thread the end of the cord through the drilled hole on the coral bead and then glue the end of the cord into the other hole to form a loop. Drill a shallow hole in the middle of the ivory piece, and attach the other cord with glue. Thread the ivory piece through the cord loop, making a beautiful decorative clasp.

Big Cuff Bracelet

ARTIST

Seth Savarick

POLYMER CLAY IS THE PERFECT MEDIUM FOR CREATING LARGER JEWELRY FORMS BECAUSE IT IS LIGHTWEIGHT. SCREENPRINTING ON POLYMER RENDERS SURFACE DESIGN WITH PRECISION AND REFINEMENT.

MATERIALS

Polymer clay: black, ultra-light, and a mixed yellow made of cadmium yellow, ecru, and white

Graph paper

2½ x 12-inch cardboard mailing tube

Glue stick

Waxed paper

PVA white craft glue

Sheet of rag paper

Polyester fiberfill

Wet/dry sandpaper in 320, 400, 600, 800 and 1000 grits

Paper towels

Screenprinting stencil in pattern of your choice made with pre-emulsion screen stencil film (follow the manufacturer's instructions to make the stencil)

High-grade artist's acrylic paint in cadmium red

Mineral oil

Paper towels

TOOLS

Scissors

Craft knife with #11 or #2 pointed blade

Steel ruler

Tissue blade or wallpaper scraper blade

Dividers

Pasta machine

Baking sheet, glazed tile, or polyester fiberfill

Squeegee (an old credit card works well)

Bone folder

PROCESS

1. To make the mold, begin by drawing two parallel lines 2½ inches apart on the graph paper. Use scissors to cut out the paper, allowing a ½-inch allowance on each side, making the strip 3½ inches wide.

2. Use the craft knife to cut the cardboard mailing tube in half. Set aside one half.

3. Use the glue stick to adhere the graph paper strip to the inside of half of the mailing tube, keeping the lines you drew perpendicular to the end of the tube.

4. Use the craft knife and steel ruler to cut the tube lengthwise, following the drawn lines on the graph paper, making the edges straight and clean. Begin by making shallow cuts with your knife followed by multiple passes. When you're done, remove the graph paper from inside the mold.

5. To make the core for your bracelet, begin by conditioning the ultra-light polymer clay. Roll it into a thick log. Use your fingers to press the log into the mold and fill it. Run the stiff tissue blade down the mold's length to trim the clay flush with the top. Carefully remove this piece from the mold without distorting it. Lay the core out on waxed paper with the flat side down. Set it aside.

6. Wrap a sheet of rag paper around the uncut piece of the cardboard mailing tube. Glue it in place. Set it aside.

(continued on page 114)

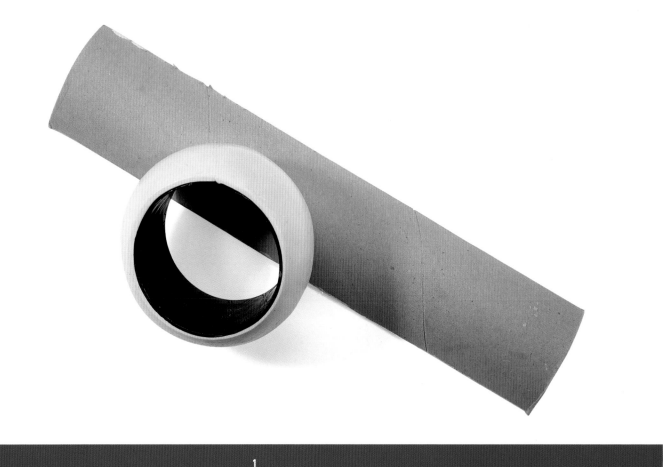

7. Use the dividers to measure the width of the bracelet core's flat side. Transfer this measurement to a sheet of graph paper and draw two corresponding parallel lines down the length of the sheet. You'll use this sheet as a cutting guide for the bracelet liner.

8. Condition the black clay and roll it into a sheet approximately ⅛-inch thick. Cut the sheet into a rectangle approximately 4 x 11 inches and place on a sheet of waxed paper.

9. Lay the black sheet down on the paper cutting guide and use a tissue/clay blade and steel ruler to cut the sheet into a strip of clay the exact width of the bracelet's core. Carefully wrap the black sheet around the mailing tube covered with rag paper so the sheet adheres to it. Keep the edges straight and square. Trim the length so the edges form a butt joint. Smooth the seam.

10. Cut one end of the ultra-light clay core squarely and cleanly. Align the core with the black clay on the mailing tube, lining up the edges to meet perfectly. Slowly wrap the core around the form, aligning the edges with the black clay. Cut the core's length to meet in a butt joint, easing the core form ends together. Gently smooth the joint's seam and fill in any gaps with additional ultra-light clay without worrying about making the seam totally smooth at this point.

11. Place the mailing tube upright in the oven on a baking sheet or glazed tile. or lay the tube on its side on a bed of polyester fiberfill. Cure the bracelet core at 275°F for two hours and allow it to cool.

12. Remove the bracelet core from the mailing tube by sliding it off with the rag paper. Remove the paper from the core (photo 1). If it sticks, remove as much as you can before soaking the core in water for about 15 minutes. Use your fingers to gently rub off any residual paper.

13. Sand the outer surface of the bracelet core with 220- or 320-grit wet/dry sandpaper. Concentrate on smoothing the butt joint seam. Carefully dry the bracelet core with paper towels. Set it aside and let it rest for 24 hours after sanding.

14. Condition the mixed yellow clay and use the pasta machine to roll it into a sheet approximately 12 x 6 inches and $\frac{1}{16}$ inch thick.

15. Use the prepared screenprint stencil and the cadmium red acrylic paint to create a surface design on the sheet of yellow polymer. To do this, place the screen stencil glossy side down on the yellow clay sheet with the long edges running perpendicular to you. Place a line of paint across the top edge of the screen, making sure to apply enough that it will fully cover the design when it is squeegeed down. Hold the squeegee at a 45° angle to the clay sheet and draw the paint down toward yourself in one smooth motion. You don't need to apply much pressure. For best results, squeegee the paint in one pass. Remove the screen stencil and immediately wash the residual paint away with cool water. Allow the paint to dry completely or approximately 15 minutes (photo 2).

16. While the clay sheet is drying, use your fingers to coat the outside of the bracelet core (not the interior) with a thin coat of PVA white glue. Let it dry. After it dries, slide the bracelet core back onto the cardboard mailing tube.

17. Trim the yellow screenprinted sheet of clay to the edge of the design. Begin at the center and carefully work out and up to the edges to upholster the core with the screenprinted sheet, turning it as you go. Take your time! Apply a very light coat of mineral oil to aid in the smoothing and easing of this outer veneer. Use a bone folder to work the

sheet into the edge where the core form meets the cardboard mailing tube. Cut the sheet to length to form a butt seam. Cut off all the scrap clay at the edge where the core meets the mailing tube.

18. Cure the veneered bracelet for 30 minutes at 275°F. Let the bracelet cool completely before removing it from the mailing tube.

19. Finish the inner edges by sanding them with 400-grit wet/dry sandpaper, taking care not to sand off the screen-printed design.

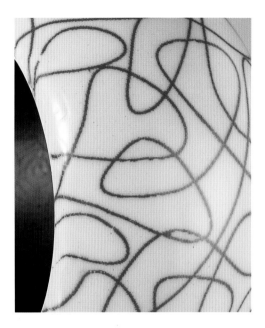

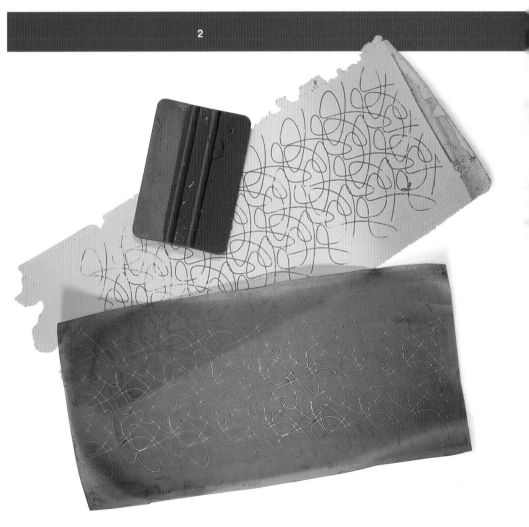

Harlequin

ARTIST

Jennifer Bezingue

Necklace, Earrings, and Bracelet

THE HUMAN EYE DELIGHTS IN CONTRAST, AND THIS DESIGN PROVIDES IT IN SEVERAL WAYS: BLACK VERSUS WHITE, GEOMETRIC VERSUS RANDOM, OPAQUE VERSUS TRANSPARENT, AND MATTE VERSUS SHINY.

MATERIALS

Polymer clay: white and black

49-strand beading wire (for necklace)

Colored glass beads

Small triangular sterling silver beads

Sterling silver tube crimp beads

Sterling silver toggle clasp

18-gauge sterling silver wire (for pendant)

20-gauge sterling silver wire (for earrings)

Sterling silver earring hooks

Strip of leather

Waxed paper

Liquid polymer clay

Polyester fiberfill

TOOLS

Pasta machine

Clay extruder with square and triangular discs

Tissue blade

Acrylic roller

Ruler

Needle tool

Bead rack and baking pins

Baking sheet

Bead board or towel

Wire cutters

Crimping pliers

Scissors

PROCESS FOR NECKLACE AND EARRINGS

1. Make a large cane from conditioned clay for each design you plan to use. Variations on the following canes are used in this project, and examples are shown in photo 1.

■ Checkerboard and triangular design canes: Use the extruder to form square and triangular lengths of clay from both black and white. To make either of these canes, tightly butt the logs of clay together, maintaining sharp corners. Use the tissue blade to cut the canes in half before reducing them two or three times.

■ Bulls-eye cane: Use the pasta machine to roll out a log of white clay (¼-inch diameter) and a separate sheet of black clay. Wrap double thicknesses of each color around the log, butting the ends of the strips, until the cane has three black stripes. (Begin with a large bulls-eye cane, since you'll use more of this design on the pieces than the others.) Roll to reduce to four or five different sizes.

(continued on page 118)

1

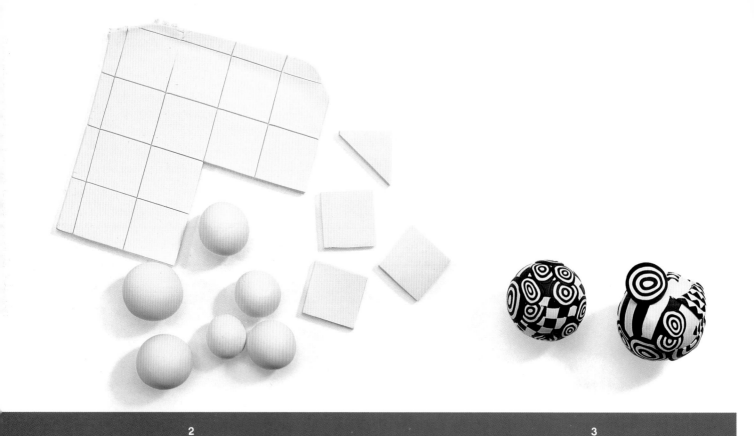

2

3

2. After each cane is assembled, use the tissue blade to cut it in half and set one piece aside. Reduce the second half one or more times so you end up with cane patterns in several sizes.

3. To create the stripes, alternately layer sheets of contrasting clay. Cut them in half, stack them, and use the acrylic roller to press the layers together. Cut them in half, stack them, and reduce them two more times to create three different sizes of stripes.

4. Roll out a sheet of white clay at the thickest setting on the pasta machine. Use the ruler and a needle tool to mark horizontal and vertical lines on the clay at ¾-inch intervals. Cut the squares apart, and cut some of them in half. Make the graduated sizes by combining 1, 1½, 2, and 2½ squares together. Roll them by hand to make round base beads (photo 2). For example, the pendant on

this necklace is made from 2½ squares of clay; the earrings are made from one.

5. To begin decorating the beads, use the tissue blade to cut thin, but easy to handle, slices from the geometric canes. Begin the design with slices from the larger ones, loosely covering the bead's surface. Press the slices into the surface of the bead as you place them. If needed, roll the bead between your palms to fully incorporate the cane slices.

6. When the surface is loosely covered, begin using slices from the smaller bulls-eye canes to overlap the edges of the geometric-patterned design canes, breaking up the design (photo 3). When the surface is completely covered, roll the beads until they're smooth and even.

7. Stick baking pins through each of the beads and place them in the bead rack to prevent flat or shiny spots after they're baked. Bake them at 275°F for 45 minutes or according to the clay manufacturer's suggestions.

8. Begin the construction of the necklace by making a pendant. (Note: If you don't know basic jewelry construction techniques, and need more information, you can learn them at local bead stores where you buy your materials.) Cut a length of 18-gauge sterling silver wire to assemble the wire-wrapped pendant. Make a wrapped loop that has a silver triangular drop bead. String silver, glass and clay beads on the wire, and make another wrapped loop at the top of the pendant. Cut off the excess wire with wire cutters.

9. Arrange the rest of the beads on a bead board or towel. String one half of the beads onto the 49-strand beading wire before adding the beaded pendant. Add the remaining beads on the other side of the necklace. Before finishing the ends, check the necklace length. Add the crimp bead and one part of the toggle clasp. Bring the end of the wire back through the crimp bead, and use crimping pliers to crush the crimp bead. Trim the wire with wire cutters. This creates a very strong necklace that won't stretch out of shape or easily come apart.

10. Make the earrings with the same construction as the pendant using 20-gauge sterling silver wire. Add an earring hook to the top loop of each.

PROCESS FOR CUFF BRACELET

1. From the sheet of leather, use scissors to cut a strip ½ inch narrower than the desired finished width, and ½ inch shorter than the circumference of your wrist. Apply a thin coat of liquid polymer clay to the rough side of the leather.

2. Roll a sheet of white clay through the pasta machine at the thickest setting. The resulting sheet should be at least 1 inch longer and wider than your leather strip. Place the clay sheet on waxed paper. Cut thin slices from canes and press the slices randomly into the sheet (photo 4). Occasionally, cover the sheet with waxed paper and burnish it until slices are completely incorporated. When it's fully patterned, roll it through the pasta machine on the thickest setting to smooth the surface.

3. Roll another sheet of white clay out on the thickest setting, and cut a strip that is ½ inch narrower than the width and length of the leather strip. Lay it over the liquid polymer clay. Press the edges of the clay strip to bevel them to the edges of the leather strip. Lay the cane-patterned sheet face up over the

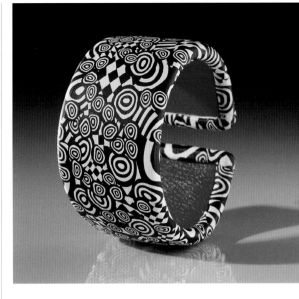

beveled clay strip, and press it firmly to ensure no air is trapped between the layers.

4. Turn the piece over and trim the edges ½ inch wider than the leather strip. Curl the edges toward the leather side. To form corners, turn the long edges first, followed by the short edges. Gently curve the leather strip into an oval shape, and place it on a fiberfill-lined baking sheet (to avoid flat or shiny spots after baking). Bake the piece at 275°F for 45 minutes or according to the clay manufacturer's suggestions.

4

Silver-Tipped Polymer Brooch

ARTIST

Julia Converse Sober

Sea creatures were the inspiration for this elegant piece. Made of a silver wire armature covered with clay, it shows off a decorative inlay of translucent clay. Sanding and buffing the final piece results in a surface as pleasing to the touch as it is to the eyes.

MATERIALS

Polymer clay: black, translucent

20-gauge sterling silver wire

Wet/dry sandpaper: 320-, 400- and 600-grit

Soft tightly-woven cloth for buffing

Brass eyelets, ⅛-inch

Cornstarch

Gold, silver, or imitation leaf

Pencil and paper

Waxed paper

TOOLS

Wire cutter

Self-locking tweezers

Flameproof surface (such as firebrick or soldering pad)

Butane pencil torch

Dust mask

Fine flat file

Pasta machine

Needle tool

Craft knife

Circular punch

Tissue blade

Acrylic rod

Chain-nose pliers

PROCESS

1. Begin by using wire cutters to cut the silver wire into four 6-inch pieces and one 8-inch piece. To burn balls on the ends of the wire, use the locking tweezers to hold one wire at a time vertically at its midpoint. Position the wire over the flameproof surface to catch any stray bits of hot metal.

2. Light the butane pencil torch and adjust the flame so the inner cone is about ½-inch long. Move the flame over the lower length of the wire until the end begins to glow orange. To make a ball, focus the blue cone of the flame slightly upwards on the tip of the wire. As the forming ball consumes the metal, it will begin to crawl slowly up the length of the wire. Remove the flame when the ball is a size you like, taking care not to melt so much metal that the ball falls off the end of the wire. If necessary, reheat the ball from the opposite side to center it on the wire.

3. When you're done, remove any resulting oxidation on the wire ends by sanding them with 320- and 400-grit wet/dry sandpaper. To restore the shine of the silver, buff the ends by hand with a soft polishing cloth.

4. To form the armature for the clay, gather the five wires into a bundle with the plain wires pointing downward. Thread a ⅛-inch brass eyelet, flared end first, over the wires. Pull this eyelet to the top of the bundle and arrange the balled ends in a pleasing variety of lengths.

5. Approximately ½ inch below the top eyelet, wrap a short piece of wire tightly around the bundle to secure it. Pull the 8-inch wire out, perpendicular to the bundle, just below the coil. (This wire will become the pin of your brooch.)

(continued on page 122)

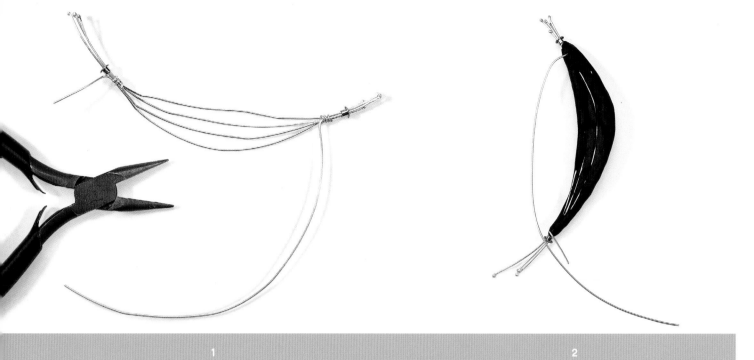

6. Arrange the four wires into a crescent shape slightly smaller than the desired size of the brooch. This will accommodate the clay form you'll build next. To secure the crescent shape and create a catch for the pin wire, coil an additional separate piece of wire tightly around the armature, approximately 1 inch from the bottom. Pull the single remaining plain wire end perpendicular to the bundle just below this coil (photo 1). The loose wire ends are now pointing out from what will become the backside of the brooch.

7. Now place the second eyelet on the plain ends of the wire. Separate the wire ends slightly so you can burn balls on the ends of them, as described in steps 2 and 3. Finish the wire ends and arrange them as you wish.

8. Next you'll cover the armature with a piece of clay cut from a black polymer sheet. Shape a ball of conditioned black clay into a crescent-shaped pad long enough to cover the front of the armature from just above the top coil to just below the bottom coil. Press the clay onto the armature, partially embedding

the wires in the clay (photo 2). Create a taper, and secure the wraps by pushing the clay from front to back around them.

9. Cover any exposed wire or low spots in the back of the base form with a smaller pad of clay. Smooth the outer form with cornstarch and compress the clay with your fingertips to secure the wires and refine your shape. (Cornstarch reduces the clay's surface tension, making it easier for you to work on the soft clay.)

10. Flatten the back of the form and refine the shape so the brooch lies flat. Smooth any seams, including the points where the clay transitions to wire. Cure this base form at 275°F for 25 minutes or according to the clay manufacturer's specifications.

11. When the base form is cool, put on a dust mask and use the fine flat file to smooth any surface bumps. Working a file in one direction will quickly refine the front curve and flatten the back of your base form. Leave the filed surface of your base form rough.

12. Roll a medium-thick sheet of black clay through your pasta machine and place the cured base form on it as a guide. Cut a crescent shape as tall as the base form and wide enough to wrap the entire form from front to back. Smooth this sheet over the form, and trim it in the back, creating a seam that runs between the pin back wires. Smooth this seam by gently "petting" the clay with the very tip of your finger from one side of the seam to the other.

13. Slide the eyelets into the clay at each tapered end and smooth the seams flush, creating a clean transition between metal and clay. Any excess clay trapped between the exposed wires and the eyelets can be removed with a needle tool after baking. Remove fingerprints by smoothing the raw form with cornstarch.

14. Trace a curved rectangle onto the front of the brooch with a needle tool, marking where the decorative cutout will be placed. Slice cleanly through the unbaked layer to the base form using a craft knife. Cut along the lines to create a frame for the decorative clay that you'll place later. Peel this clay piece away and set it aside for later reference. Cure the form again at 275°F for 25 minutes or according to the clay manufacturer's suggestions.

15. To begin the decorative inlay, roll out a sheet of black clay the same thickness as your framing layer. Roll translucent clay into several thinner small sheets. Apply pieces of gold, silver, or other colored metal leaf to the translucent sheets and run each through the pasta machine. The clay protects the fragile leaf from flaking off or tarnishing and adds surface depth. Crackle effects can be achieved by running the leafed sheet of clay through successively smaller settings on your pasta machine. Change directions each time you run it through the machine to make primarily square and regular patterns, or run it through the same way several times to create horizontal fracture lines.

16. Use a circular punch as well as a tissue blade to cut a variety of shapes from each leafed sheet. With the leaf side down, layer these shapes onto the black base sheet to seal the leafed surface between the black and translucent clays. Cover the final collaged sheet of black and translucent clay with waxed paper and flatten it using an acrylic rod. Remove the waxed paper and run the flattened sheet through successively thinner settings on your pasta machine to the same thickness as the black framing layer.

17. Use a pencil and paper to trace around the black clay rectangle you cut out earlier. Cut this shape out of the interior of the paper, leaving an empty rectangle in the center of it. Position this paper frame over your collaged sheet to find a pleasing design and set the frame

in place directly on the sheet. Use the craft knife to cut the sheet carefully along the inside edges of the frame. Remove the frame and pull the unused sheet of clay away from the cut shape (photo 3).

18. Position the decorative cut shape into the recessed area on the brooch (photo 4) and press the edges flush with the frame. Cover the shape with a bit of waxed paper and press from the center to the outside edges to remove any trapped air and smooth the surface. Remove the waxed paper and bake your brooch one last time at the same temperature and for the same amount of time.

19. Cut 320-, 400-, and 600-grit sandpaper into smaller squares and soak them in slightly soapy water while your piece cures. When the brooch cools off, sand the whole surface with 320-grit

paper until smooth. Occasionally rinse off the paper with water. Repeat with 400- and 600-grit sandpaper.

20. To finish the catch of your brooch, use the chain-nose pliers to grasp the pin wire approximately ⅛ inch from the back of the brooch, bending it so it lies parallel to the back of the brooch. Form the catch by grasping the end of the bottom wire with your pliers and curling it to the right, forming a U-shaped loop to hold the pin in place. Trim this wire to keep the catch close to the pin for comfortable wear. Taper and sharpen the end of the pin wire using a flat file, then curve it to follow the graceful lines of your brooch. Refine the catch with pliers as needed so it securely holds the pin wire.

21. Finally, buff your piece by hand with a tightly woven fabric to bring out a deep, satiny sheen.

Enamel Choker

ARTIST

Julia Converse Sober

SOLDERED SILVER END CAPS ADD A PROFESSIONAL LOOK TO THIS BRIGHTLY COLORED, LUMINOUS BEAD DECORATED WITH A LIQUID CLAY TRANSFER. A FEW MATERIALS FROM A JEWELRY SUPPLIER AND SOME PRACTICE WILL OPEN NEW DOORS TO CREATING SOLDERED ELEMENTS FOR YOUR CLAY WORK

MATERIALS

24-gauge sterling silver strip

320- and 400-grit sandpaper

Paste flux

Easy and super-easy silver wire solder

Film canister cap or other small container

24-gauge sterling silver sheet

Soldering pad or firebrick

Liquid polymer clay

Colored pencils

Photocopied images (for transfers)

Small piece of framing glass

Thick white glue

Silver leaf

Sheet of paper

18-gauge sterling silver square wire

Translucent polymer clay

Cyanoacrylate glue

Silver omega or snake chain

Embossing stylus or comb

TOOLS

Wire cutters

Flat hand file

Stainless steel fine-tip tweezers

Butane pencil torch

Round-nose and chain-nose pliers

Jeweler's saw frame with saw blades (size 3/0)

Flat nylon paintbrush

Small natural-bristle brush

Toner photocopier

Scissors

Flat nylon paintbrush

Comb or ball-end stylus

Pasta machine

Craft knife

Ruler

Center punch

Hammer

Pin vise and bits

PROCESS FOR END CAPS

1. To create the silver end caps, the first step is soldering simple bands, which are then soldered to a sheet of silver. These are used as the bezel portion of the end caps. Begin by using the wire cutters to cut two pieces of 2-inch-long sterling strip. Bend the silver strip into an oval with your fingers, pressing the ends past each other and butting them together to make a tension fit on one long flat side. Use the file or sandpaper to file the seam to meet perfectly, and apply a dab of paste flux to both ends.

2. Clean the easy wire solder by pulling one end through a small piece of 320-grit sandpaper. Using wire cutters, snip small chips from the end of the wire solder onto a dab of flux placed in a film canister cap or other small container.

3. Add two tiny chips of solder to the band using your fine-tip tweezers, overlapping them against both sides of the seam. Using the butane pencil torch, heat the entire band in a circular motion, concentrating the flame across the seam when the piece glows red. Remove the heat immediately when the solder flows in a bright line across the seam.

4. Sand the edges of both bands flat in a circular motion over 320-grit sandpaper placed on a smooth, flat surface. This keeps the edges of the band perfectly even for further soldering.

5. Shape the bands into matching pointed ovals using round-nose and chain-nose pliers. Trace rough outlines of both bands with a pencil on the 24-gauge sterling silver sheet.

6. Use a jeweler's saw, pictured in photo 1, to cut ovals from the silver sheet, leaving a ⅛-inch border around each outline. These saws are designed to cut on the pull stroke and require a light touch to avoid breaking blades. Begin by inserting a blade in the saw's frame with the teeth facing forward and down from the saw's front edge. Tighten the blade in the top clamp first, adjust the saw length if necessary, and insert the blade into the bottom clamp. Pull the open ends of the saw frame together slightly and tighten the bottom clamp, leaving some tension on the blade. Anchor the silver sheet in place on a bench pin.

7. Keep the saw blade vertical, moving smoothly up and down as you cut. Rotate the sheet instead of the saw, moving slowly along the sheet to follow the lines of curves. If the sheet distorts while cutting, place the cut shape flat on a hard, flat and hammer it flat for a perfect fit with the bezel band.

8. Sand the surface of the silver sheet with 320-grit sandpaper to clean it and apply a light coating of paste with a small natural-bristle paintbrush. Add additional flux to the edges of each oval band. Center the bands onto the oval sheets making sure there's a perfect flat fit, and place the whole works on a soldering pad.

9. Prepare and clean your wire solder by pulling it repeatedly through folded sandpaper. Use your wire cutters to snip small chips into a dab of flux. Using your fine-tip tweezers, place six to eight tiny fluxed solder chips evenly around the interior of each band. Each chip should touch both the bezel band and the underlying sheet.

10. When all pieces are fitted in place, light the butane torch and adjust the flame so the blue cone in the center of the flame is approximately 1-inch long. Starting in the center, heat the whole piece, working slowly in and out in a circular motion. Keep the flame moving over the entire piece until the flux bubbles and runs clear.

11. If the solder chips change position in the bubbling flux, remove the flame and nudge any wandering chips back into place with the fine-point tweezers. Relight your torch and reheat the entire piece as before.

12. When the entire piece glows bright orange and the flux is clear and glassy, concentrate the flame in a circling motion around the outside edge of the seam. Solder will flow into a bright silver line around each band, securing it to the metal sheet. Remove the heat immediately after the solder flows! If your piece doesn't completely solder the first time, clean the seam with sandpaper, apply more flux and solder chips, and reheat as above. Let the pieces air-cool.

13. Use the jeweler's saw to trim the excess sheet from around each bezel band (photo 1). Cut close to (but not touching) the bezel edges to avoid marring the silver bands. After cutting, file away the remaining rough sheet overhang using the flat hand file held parallel to the sides of each band. Move the file only in a forward direction to avoid clogging the file teeth. Remove material gradually around the band until the solder seam disappears. If gaps appear in your seams as you file, clean your piece again and solder, as above.

14. Finally, file the outside bezel band surface to remove any oxidation and sand the entire outside of the end cap with 320-grit sandpaper.

PROCESS FOR BEAD

1. Next, you'll use liquid clay and colored pencils to create a flexible transfer to wrap around a clay bead form. When selecting imagery for this bead, use photocopied images at least as wide as the desired bead size with enough length to wrap around the entire bead perimeter (or at least 2 inches). Use a toner photocopier to copy your images. Use colored pencils in varied and contrasting shades to fill it in completely.

2. Deposit color heavily on the paper and over the toner lines, since the pigment acts as a release once the transfer is cured, preventing the paper from sticking. In addition to coloring the image, fill in a generous border that will be trimmed away later, ensuring a complete, usable image after curing.

3. Use scissors to cut the colored image from the paper, leaving a border of plain paper around the colored edges for easier handling. Use the flat nylon paintbrush to brush a medium-thick layer of liquid clay directly on the colored image. The liquid clay should be just thick enough to blur the lines and mute the colors of the image.

4. Apply the image to the piece of glass, trapping the liquid clay between it and the paper (photo 2). To minimize air bubble formation, slowly roll the coated image onto the piece of glass from one side of the image to the other. Turn the entire glass over to find air bubbles, which appear as dark spots in the milky liquid clay layer. Use the side of your finger to carefully ease any air bubbles from the center to the edges of the paper. Be patient as you do this slowly, keeping the side of your finger flat against the paper.

5. Once the air bubbles are removed, turn the glass over again and bake the transfer at 300 to 325°F for approximately 10 minutes. Liquid clay requires higher temperatures to cure properly and will burn before you know it, so keep an eye on it. Your transfer is properly cured when the excess liquid clay around the paper edges is completely clear.

(continued on page 128)

1

2

3   4   5

6. Remove the cured transfer from the oven and let the glass cool for several minutes. Peel off the transfer and remove the paper backing, beginning at the outside edges. Stretch the cured transfer paper side up between your thumbs and forefingers, tearing the paper. A properly cured transfer is strong and flexible. Carefully remove any excess bits of stuck paper with a moist fingertip to avoid scratching off the transferred pigment.

7. Before adding the textured glue layer, trim the rough edges from around your image and stick it back onto the piece of glass, shiny side down. Using your finger or a flat brush, apply a fairly thin layer of thick white glue to the pigment side of your transfer. Using a comb or ball-end stylus, pull lines through the glue to add as much texture as you like. Let the glue dry clear before continuing.

8. To add an enamel-like luminescence to your transfer, exhale over the entire dried glue surface to reactivate the

adhesive and apply a sheet of silver leaf. Cover the leaf with a sheet of paper and burnish the metal surface into any recessed areas of the glue texture. When the leaf sheet is completely adhered to your transfer, turn it over and admire the brilliance of your colors (photo 3).

9. Next you'll make the bead form, which is cured in two stages. The first stage establishes the form, allowing for refinement after curing. The second stage fits the bead form to the end cap, leaving room for the transfer to be inserted after a second curing. Begin this process by using your soldered end caps as a sizing and symmetry guide for forming a ball of translucent clay into a flattened oval. The final bead form should fit loosely into the caps, with a slight space between the bead surface and the inner bezel band (photo 4). This allows room for the later addition of your transfer.

10. Bake this initial bead form at 275°F for 25 minutes or according to the clay manufacturer's instructions. When the bead is cool, use a flat file to remove and smooth any bumps or high spots in the surface so the bead has a smooth and even curve on both sides.

11. To securely attach the transfer piece and end caps later, one more baking step is required. Use the pasta machine to roll out a thin sheet of translucent clay. Using your end caps as cutters, press out small ovals from the sheet (photo 5). Secure the thin clay firmly into the base of each end cap. Place the initial bead form between the end caps and center it once again. Before baking, cut two pieces of square 18-gauge silver wire to the same width as the finished form. Fit the wires into the end caps at the top and bottom edges of the form. Trim excess material away from the top and bottom of the form with a craft knife or file. Firmly press the whole assembly together again to set the bead and wires into the raw clay, and bake the entire assembled piece again for the full curing time.

12. Remove the end caps and wires from your cooled bead form. Use a ruler and pencil to mark centerlines on the interior of each end cap at the tallest and widest points of the oval bezel band. Position the tip of your center punch at the center point of each bezel and tap it lightly with a hammer to make a small dent where the hole will be. Center a drill bit large enough to accommodate the neck chain in the dent. Use a pin vise fitted with a bit the size of your chain to carefully and slowly drill through each end cap. Sand the end caps one last time with 320-grit sandpaper to create a brushed-metal finish. If you want to make it even shinier, sand it with 400- and 600-grit paper and buff with a polishing cloth.

13. Cut your transfer with scissors into a strip to fit between the raised outside edges of the finished polymer bead form. Wrap this strip around the bead form, adjusting the design until you like it, and then trim the strip to size. Apply a small amount of white glue to the recessed area in the base bead and let dry until tacky.

14. Roll the transfer strip slowly onto the bead form starting and ending at the top point of the oval form. Trim the transfer strip as necessary so the ends fit flush. To secure the transfer onto the bead while the glue bonds, wrap the bead tightly with a strip of paper and tape it in place. Let the glue cure for a few hours or overnight.

15. To finish assembling your bead, remove the paper and set the wires in place at the top and bottom on the bead form, securing and covering the seam. With wires in place, test-fit the bead form to the end caps to make sure all the pieces are oriented and fit properly (photo 6). Press the end caps securely in place and drill a hole through the polymer bead form. For best results, drill towards the center from both sides until the hole meets and runs through. Run the drill bit through the entire bead hole a few additional times to clean out and smooth the interior.

16. Finally, glue the end caps in place, one side at a time. Remove the cap and apply a small amount of cyanoacrylate glue in each interior corner. Carefully fit the cap back onto the bead form and press it firmly in place for 15 seconds before gluing the other side.

17. When the bead form is secure and finished, thread it onto a simple silver chain.

6

Medal of Honor

ARTIST

Wendy Wallin Malinow

This unusual pin— a fresh take on the medal of honor—is part of a series of pieces created to celebrate daily life. This small house-shaped shrine contains found objects encased in resin.

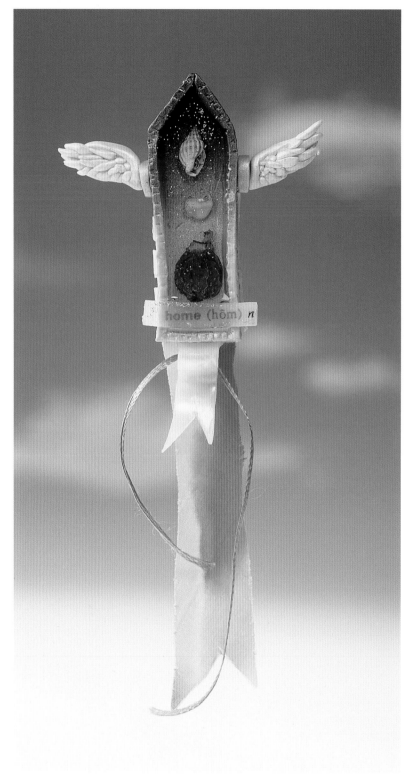

MATERIALS

Polymer clay: range of colors, pearl, and
   translucent

Pearlized pigment powder

20-gauge copper or silver wire

Polyester fiberfill

Gin (for solvent)

PVA glue

Small found objects

Two-part epoxy resin

Pin back

TOOLS

Pasta machine

Ruler

Tissue blade

Texture plate or sandpaper

Clay shaping tools

Wire cutters

Round-nose pliers

Toner-based photocopier

Spoon or other burnishing tool

Small paintbrush

Heat gun (optional)

PROCESS

1. Mix two colors of clay with a bit of pearl clay to add sheen to the colors. Create a Skinner Blend about 6 x 6 inches on the thickest setting of your pasta machine.

2. Use a ruler and pencil to draw a layout outlining two side panels and a corresponding house shape (photo 1). The side panels measure approximately 2 3/4 x 3/4 inches. The central piece, or backside of the house, measures 2 3/4 inches high at the top of the roof and 3/4 inches wide. The base of the piece measures 3/4 inches wide by 5/8 inches high. The fold line for the panels, indicated by the dotted line, is about 1/2 inch from the top.

3. Use this template as a guide to cut the two side panels, the base, and the backside with mitered roofline. Place the pieces on a piece of paper.

4. Apply texture with a texture plate or sandpaper to the outside and inside of the panels. Handle them carefully and don't press them too hard. Place the panels back down on the layout to check for distortion (photo 1).

5. Use the small paintbrush to add pearlized pigment powder to the textured clay.

6. Assemble the side panels and backside of the house, curving the roofline to fit. Add the base piece and press the seams together.

(continued on page 132)

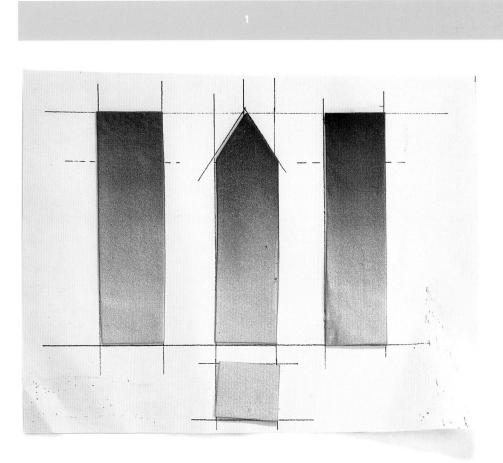

2

Gently rub off the excess white paper with your finger. Cure the pieces, and remove the remaining paper residue more vigorously.

10. Trim the strips and adhere them to the sides of the house, saving one saying for the front of the house. Use a remaining scrap of translucent clay to form a ribbon for the bottom of the medal. Cut out the strip of clay and bend it into an undulating shape. Attach it to the base.

11. On a support of fiberfill, cure the house according to the clay manufacturer's directions.

12. Roll small snakes of clay from the blend and smooth them into the bottom and corners inside the house to strengthen the joins. Cure the house again and let it cool.

13. Place found objects of your choice inside the house. (This particular piece has a small dried rose hip, a baby tooth, and a shell.) Use white, archival glue to attach them.

14. Following the manufacturer's instructions, mix a small amount of two-part epoxy resin and fill the inside of the house with it. Follow carefully all safety rules and precautions and ventilate your work area well. Do not allow fumes to linger.

15. If air bubbles form, you can pass lightly over the resin with the heat gun, holding it about 15 inches above the piece. For small numbers of bubbles, use a toothpick to remove them. Allow the piece to rest for about 24 hours.

16. Attach ribbons to the bottom wire loop.

17. Attach the pin back with a bit of polymer clay (see page 20).

7. Condition a small amount of pearl clay and shape it into small wings. Embed a wire into each wing to strengthen it. Affix the wings to the sides of the house box with the wire (photo 2). Place the piece on polyester fiberfill, supporting the wings.

8. Use the round-nose pliers to form a tiny round wire loop wire and push it into the center of the base.

9. To make text images to decorate the piece, copy reverse-image text on a toner-based photocopier. Cut the words into desired sayings. Roll out a thin, translucent sheet of clay. Place the text facedown on the clay and burnish it well with a spoon or other tool. Use your finger to coat and saturate the back of the paper with gin. Blot it if too much liquid remains on the paper. Burnish it again. Be careful not to use too much pressure. Carefully roll the paper off the clay.

Sea Fantasy Necklace

ARTIST

Wendy Wallin Malinow

THIS TOUR DE FORCE OF CLAY SCULPTING SHOWS OFF A SAMPLER OF INVENTIVE BEADS INSPIRED BY AQUATIC FORMS. SUCH SIMPLE SHAPES ALLOW YOU FREEDOM TO CONCENTRATE ON COLOR, SHAPE, AND TEXTURE. USE THIS FINAL PROJECT AS A SPRINGBOARD FOR ADVENTURESOME PIECES.

MATERIALS

Polymer clay: various colors (such as turquoise, purple, and a range of blues complimented by bright accents such as yellow, pink, and orange), pearlescent, translucent

Metallic pigment powders

18-gauge wire on spool

Polyester fiberfill

Strong, thick nylon thread

Cyanoacrylate glue

TOOLS

Pasta machine

Needle tool or awl

Clay shaping tools

Tissue blade

Rigid wire rods (thin knitting needles or heavier-weight wire)

Pliers

PROCESS

1. Mix the various clay colors with pearlescent clay.

2. Make assorted simple canes from thin sheets of colored clay wrapped around translucent snakes to use for surface decoration. Use thicker slices to create a relief effect. To make spikes, roll out small balls of clay, graduated in size, and then roll the sides with your finger (photo 1).

3. Each bead begins with a simple shape (photo 2). After you make each shape, pierce it with 2- to 5-inch curved lengths of 18-gauge sturdy wire, unless stipulated otherwise. Leave the wire in for baking. (Note that it is often easier to pierce the base bead with the wire before adding delicate surface details.)

4. Brush on a coat of pearlized metallic powder for highlights before curing the beads on polyester fiberfill.

5. The following descriptions are suggestions for making some of the beads shown. Use them to get your imagination going, and then cut loose on your own! Refer to the photo on page 133 as you read the descriptions.

■ Donut-shaped beads (bottom center): Roll a ¼-inch thick snake and shape it into a donut. Seal the edges together well. Roll a tube of clay in a contrasting color and cut it into pieces ⅛ to ⅜ inches long. Pierce these small tubes with a needle tool or awl. Twist them and apply them to the donut while still on the tool. If you wish, roll and add very tiny balls from a contrasting color to cover the surface between the tubes. (This is a very time-consuming process, but the textural results are wonderful.)

■ Bead with wispy tentacles (lower right): Form a base bead out of a solid

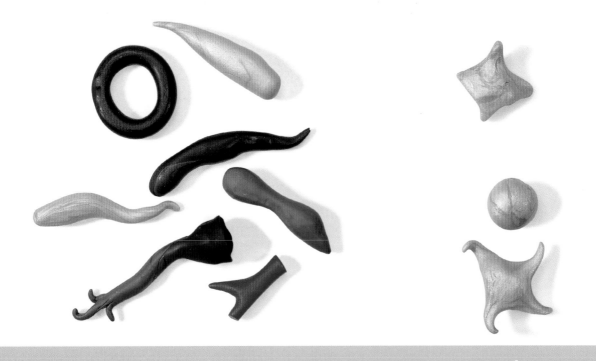

color. Roll out a small piece of Skinner Blend on a middle thickness of your pasta machine. Cut it into multiple thin strips and roll these into tiny snakes. Apply the snakes to the base bead in a layered fashion, curling them to create a feeling of surface movement.

■ Starfish beads (upper right): Roll small balls of clay. Pull out two, three, or four points of clay from each ball. Roll them to even them out. Slightly elongate and curl the points (photo 3). Embellish them with canes or dots of clay and roll these pieces into the surface.

■ Squid bead (upper right): To make the cap on the bead, roll three balls of graduated sizes from pearlized colored clay. Flatten the balls slightly and stack them on top of each other. Decorate the cap with small ⅛-inch balls pressed on the surface. Use a shaping tool to hollow out the bottom of the cap. From a Skinner Blend, roll out about seven to nine tapered snakes of different lengths. Group them and add them to the bot-

tom of the cap. Add small balls of contrasting clay to a few of the snakes.

■ Amorphous veneered bead (upper right, to left of squid): Make a base shape from a solid color. Add a decorated thin veneer of clay to the sides. Add small balls and spikes of clay to the remaining surface.

■ Coral beads (throughout necklace): Roll a snake from red clay and fork the ends of it, truncating the pieces to create different shapes that look natural.

■ Incised "pocket" bead (upper left): Make a base shape out of scrap clay. Roll out a Skinner Blend on the next-to-thinnest pasta machine setting. Wrap the blended clay around the shape. Cut a slit in the middle of it and make a depression inside. Roll a snake from contrasting clay and place it along the edges of the depression. Fill the hole with assorted small shapes such as tubes, balls, and spikes. Add texture and small snake decorations to the rest of the bead.

■ Plantlike tube beads (throughout necklace): Place a small lump of clay on a rigid, straight wire rod. Roll the clay out until ⅛-inch thick. Add balls of clay to the tube to create projections (photo 4). Add metallic powder, and gently pull the bead off the wire. Bend it slightly and place it on a baking sheet on polyester fiberfill. For a cleaner look, trim the ends after curing.

■ Thin heishi beads (throughout necklace): Roll ⅛-inch clay tubes about 6 to 9 inches long and cure them on straight wire on top of a baking tray. After cured, twist them slightly and pull the tubes from the wire. Use a sharp clay blade to cut thin slices from the tube.

6. To string the beads, remove any wires from them. If needed, use pliers to twist the wire to remove the beads. String the beads on the nylon thread. Knot the thread, and glue the knot. Clip the ends of the thread. When the glue is dry, pull the knot inside the closest bead to bury it.

Judy Kuskin
Maggie's Farm, 2004
24 inches long (61 cm)
Polymer clay, fine and sterling
silver, precious metal clay

PHOTOS © DOUG YAPLE

David Forlano
Rose Pin, 2005
3¾ x 3½ x ¾ inches
(9.5 x 8.9 x 1.9 cm)
Sterling silver, polymer clay

PHOTO © ROBERT DIAMANTE

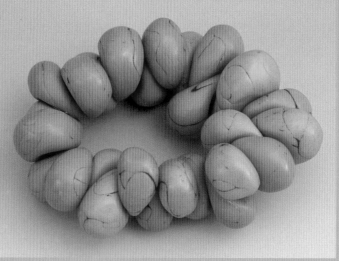

Sybille Hamilton
Pod Bracelet, 2002
1 x 3¾ x 2½ inches
(2.5 x 9.5 x 6.4 cm)
Polymer clays, acrylic paint

PHOTO © LAURA TIMMINS

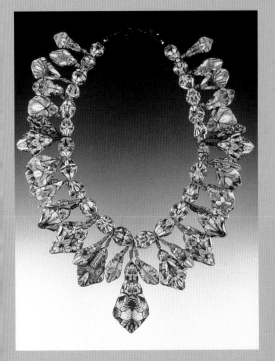

Mary Grandy
Flower Cluster Pendant Necklace, 2004
2 x 2⅝ x ¾ inches (5 x 6.7 x 1.9 cm)
Polymer clay, rubber cord; cane technique

Annabelle Fisher
Necklace in Black and White, 1999
22 inches long (55.9 cm)
Polymer clay; millefiori

Elise Winters
Triple Flair Brooch, 2002
2½ x 3½ x ¼ inches (6.4 x 8.9 x
0.6 cm)
Polymer clay, crazed acrylic, mica

Kathleen Dustin
Windblown Bracelet, 2005
3 x 2½ inches (7.6 x 6.4 cm)
Polymer clay, gold leaf lamella;
image transfer, layered,
carved, backfilled, baked,
sanded, polished

Martha Aleo
Mixed Media Bracelet, 2004
Focal bead, 1¾ x 2¾ inches (4.4 x 7 cm)
Polymer clay, sterling silver, Balinese and
sterling silver beads; cane techniques,
coiled, fabricated clasp and findings
PHOTOS © ARTIST

Grace Stokes
Pendant, 2004
2¾ x 1¾ x 21 inches
(7 x 4.4 x 53.3 cm)
Sterling silver, polymer clay,
fine silver bezel, 22- and
14-karat gold, glass beads
PHOTO © KEVIN OLDS

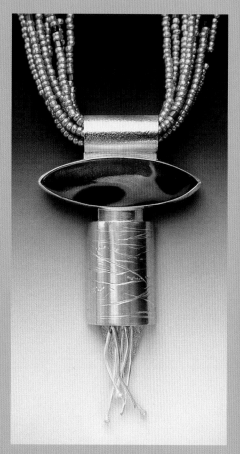

Sandra McCaw
Untitled, 2005
2 x ½ inches (5 x 1.3 cm)
Polymer clay, gold leaf
PHOTO © ROBERT DIAMANTE

Ginny Henley
Somewhere Between Chaos and Control, 2005
Beads, 1 x ¾ inch (2.5 x 1.9 cm)
Polymer clay, glass spacer beads;
cane technique, joined, cut,
backed, trimmed

Pier & Penina
Breaking Apart, 2005
1¼ x 2¼ inches
(3.2 x 5.7 cm)
Polymer clay;
cane technique

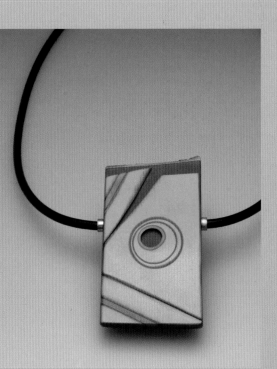

Cynthia Toops
Moss Brooch, 2004
1¼ x 4 x ½ inches (3.2 x 10.2 x 1.3 cm)
Polymer clay threads, steel pin back

Judy Kuskin
Travelin', 2004
8 ½ inches long (21.6 cm)
Polymer clay, fine and sterling silver;
fabricated hinges
PHOTO © DOUG YAPLE

Mary J. Lind
Beauty Under Glass Bracelet,
2005
6 ½ to 8 x ½ inches
(16.5 x 20.3 x 1.3 cm)
Polymer clay, filigree ornament,
metallic paint, cabochons, sterling
silver wire; texturized, punched,
baked, glued, wrapped
PHOTO © ARTIST

Victoria James
Basket Necklace, 2004
6 ½ x 1 ½ inches (16.5 x 3.8 cm)
Polymer clay, O-rings;
painted, twined, extruded,
cane embellishments
PHOTO © RICHARD REID

Steven Ford
Multi-Colored Urchin Pin, 2005
3 x 3 x ¾ inches
(7.6 x 7.6 x 1.9 cm)
Polymer clay, sterling silver
PHOTO © ROBERT DIAMANTE

Grace Stokes
Pendant, 2005
3 ¼ x 1 ½ x 20 inches
(8.3 x 3.8 x 50.8 cm)
Sterling silver, polymer clay inserts,
fine silver bezels, freshwater pearls;
glass bead granulation, bezel set
PHOTO © KEVIN OLDS

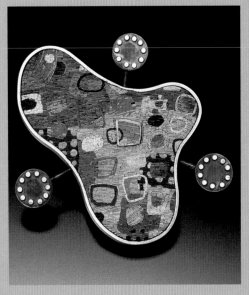

Cynthia Toops
Untitled, 2004
2 ¾ x 3 x ¼ inches
(7 x 7.6 x 0.6 cm)
Polymer clay, sterling
silver; mosaic
Metal work by
Chuck Domitrovich
PHOTO © DOUG YAPLE

Margaret Regan
Blue Ball Necklace, 2004
Beads, ¾ x ¾ x ¾ inches (1.9 x 1.9 x 1.9 cm)
Polymer clay, sterling silver, rubber, self-clasp; millefiori
PHOTO © HAP SAKWA

Elise Winters
Drop Earrings, 2001
1 ½ x ½ x ½ inches
(3.8 x 1.3 x 1.3 cm)
Polymer clay, crazed acrylic,
14-karat vermeil

PHOTO © RALPH GABRINER

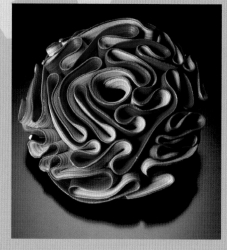

Steven Ford
Ribbon Pin, 2005
3 x 3 x ¾ inches
(7.6 x 7.6 x 1.9 cm)
Polymer clay, sterling silver
PHOTO © ROBERT DIAMANTE

Louise Fischer Cozzi
Shield Line Earrings, 2003
⅜ x ⅞ x ³⁄₃₂ inches
(0.95 x 2.2 x 0.23 cm)
Polymer clay, bronzing powders,
brass/niobium ear wires; etched,
painted, penciled
PHOTO © GEORGE POST

Terry Kovalcik
Egret, 2004
1³⁄₁₆ x 2 x ⅛ inches (3 x 5 x 0.3 cm)
Precious metal clay, polymer clay bi-cone
bead, sterling wire, cord; carved, baked
Polymer clay egret inlay created by
Corrin Jacobsen Kovalcik
PHOTO © CORRIN JACOBSEN KOVALCIK

Merrie Buchsbaum
Three-Beaded Necklace, 2003
Beads, 1½ inches (3.8 cm)
Transparent polymer clay, sterling
and gold foil, metallic powders,
sterling cable; cane technique,
hand-polished
PHOTO © JOHN POLAK

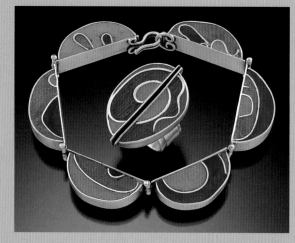

Tracy Deming
Untitled, 2004
Bracelet, 7½ x 1 inches
(19 x 2.5 cm)
Ring, 1 x ¾ inches
(2.5 x 1.9 cm)
Sterling silver, polymer
clay; fabricated
PHOTO © ARTIST

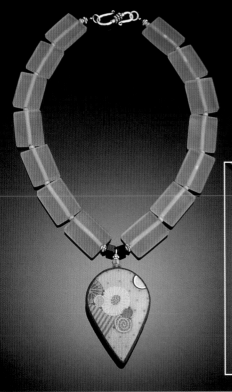

Angie Wiggins
Necklace, 2005
20 inches (50.8 cm)
Polymer clay, resin beads,
silver beads, glass beads;
cane technique, lamination, impression
PHOTOS © TAYLOR DABNEY

Tracy Deming
Untitled, 2002
¾ x 1¼ inches (1.9 x 3.2 cm)
Sterling silver, polymer clay; fabricated
PHOTO © LARRY SANDERS

Kathleen Dustin
Preraphealite Pin, 2005
3 x 1½ inches (7.6 x 3.8 cm)
Polymer clay, gold leaf lamella;
image transfer, layered,
carved, backfilled, baked,
sanded, polished
PHOTO © ROBERT DIAMANTE

Wendy Wallin Malinow
Party in a Box, 2004
20 x 4 x ¾ inches
(50.8 x 10.2 x 1.9 cm)
Sterling silver, polymer
clay, sterling boxes; fabricated, soldered, inlaid
PHOTO © COURTNEY FRISSE

Cynthia Toops
Blue Tubes Bracelet, 2004
3¾ x 2½ x 1½ inches
(9.5 x 6.4 x 3.8 cm)
Polymer clay, sterling
silver; formed, cut,
embedded, baked

PHOTO © ROGER SCHREIBER

Pier & Penina
Floating Squares Cuff, 2005
1 x 8¼ x ³⁄₁₆ inches
(2.5 x 21 x 0.5 cm)
Polymer clay; cut, layered,
mica shift

PHOTO © ARTISTS

Carol Blackburn
Beaded Necklace, 2003
17 x 1⅝ x ½ inches
(43 x 4 x 1.2 cm)
Polymer clay, glitter;
hand-shaped

PHOTOS © ARTIST

Catherine Verdiere
Galets D'été, 2005
Central bead, 2³⁄₁₆ x 2³⁄₁₆ inches
(5.5 x 5.5 cm)
Polymer clay, chalk, silver foil,
glass beads; cane techniques,
sanded, polished

PHOTO © PHILIPPE DENEUFVE

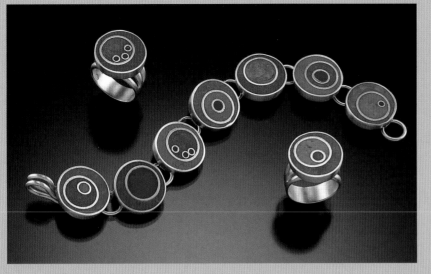

Tracy Deming
Untitled, 2004
7 ½ x 1 inches (19 x 2.5 cm)
Sterling silver, polymer clay;
fabricated
PHOTO © LARRY SANDERS

Jeffrey Lloyd Dever
Atlantis, 2005
2¾ x 1⅜ x ½ inches
(6.9 x 3.5 x 1.3 cm)
Fabricated polymer clay
hollow forms, drilled and
backfilled; glass head
pins, steel wire
PHOTO ©
GREGORY R. STALEY

Merrie Buchsbaum
Cabochon Bracelet, 2004
7 inches (17.8 cm)
Transparent polymer clay,
ground herbs, sterling silver,
sterling/copper-gold foil,
metallic powders; cane
technique, hand-polished
PHOTO © JOHN POLAK

Barbara A. McGuire
Wild World, 2005
3 x 1 inches (7.6 x 2.5 cm)
Turquoise, black coral;
mokume gane
PHOTO © ARTIST

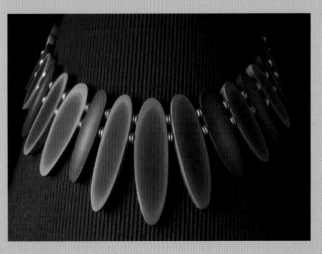

Victoria James
Tiny Faux Ivory Vessel, 2005
1³⁄₁₆ x ⅞ x ¾ inches
(3 x 2.2 x 1.9 cm)
Polymer clay, rubber cord,
O-rings; hand-built over
mold, molded decorations
PHOTO © ARTIST

Sandra McCaw
Winter Leaf Bracelet, 2005
9 inches long (22.9 cm)
Translucent polymer clay, gold leaf
PHOTO © ROBERT DIAMANTE

Cynthia Toops
Life Saver Ring #2, 2001
1½ x 1¼ inches (3.8 x 3.2 cm)
Polymer clay, sterling silver,
crystal; mosaic
Metalwork by
Chuck Domitrovich
PHOTOS © WERNER BONITZ

Annette Duburg
Untitled, 2005
8⅝ x 2 inches (22 x 5 cm)
Polymer clay, acrylic paint,
rubber cord; imprint
PHOTO © OTTO HEŸST

Louise Fischer Cozzi
Pinwheel Pin, 2004
MISSING DIMENSIONS
Polymer clay; etched,
painted, penciled
PHOTO © RALPH GABRINER

Annabelle Fisher
Basket Weave, 2001
3 x ¾ x ⅛ inches
(7.6 x 1.9 x 0.3 cm)
Polymer clay; millefiori
PHOTO © ROBERT DIAMANTE

Kay Bonitz
Untitled, 2005
18 x 1¼ x ⅜ inches
(45.7 x 3.2 x 0.95 cm)
Polymer clay, gold-filled
spacer beads; mokume gane
PHOTO © WERNER BONITZ

SL Savarick
Swashes Inro, 2004
3½ x 2½ x ¾ inches
(8.9 x 6.4 x 1.9 cm)
Polymer, liquid polymer clay,
14-karat gold metallic powder,
mica powder, silk cord;
screenprinted
PHOTO © ROBERT DIAMANTE

Bianca Terranova
Fayum Woman I & II, 2004
Approximately 3 x 1 x 2⅛ inches
(7.6 x 2.5 x 5.1 cm)
Translucent liquid polymer clay,
24-karat gold leaf; image transfer
PHOTO © ARTIST

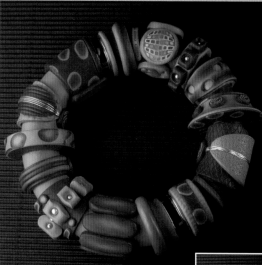

Kathleen Dustin
Victorian Circle Pin, 2005
2½ x 2 inches (6.4 x 5 cm)
Polymer clay, gold leaf lamella; image transfer, layered,
carved, backfilled, baked,
sanded, polished
PHOTO © ROBERT DIAMANTE

Catherine Verdiere
Lune Bleue, 2004
2⁷⁄₁₆ x 3¹⁵⁄₁₆ x 1³⁄₁₆ (6 x 10 x 3 cm)
Polymer clay, wire armature, silver
thread, beads, magnetic clasps
PHOTOS © PHILIPPE DENEUFVE

Cynthia Toops
Rolodex Bracelet, 2003
4 x 1½ inches
(10.2 x 3.8 cm)
Polymer clay, steel spring; rolled,
baked, hand cut, punched

Catherine Verdiere
Soleil Bleu, 2004
Central bead, 2¾ x ¹³⁄₁₆ inches (7 x 2 cm)
Polymer clay; sanded

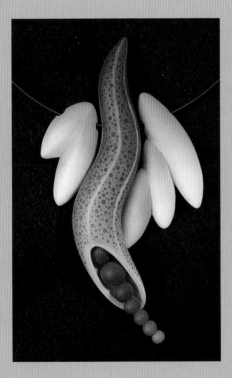

Jeffrey Lloyd Dever
Flora—The Seduction, 2004
4½ x 2½ x ⅝ inches
(11.5 x 6 x 1.6 cm)
Fabricated polymer clay
hollow forms, drilled, carved,
and backfilled; anodized
niobium cable, wire

Maura Muir Wilson
Moonscape, 2005
19 x 1 x ⅛ inches
(48.3 x 2.5 x 0.3 cm)
Polymer clay, glass beads,
precious metal clay toggle;
gradient blend, mica shift,
sanded, polished

ABOUT THE ARTISTS

Jennifer Bezingue
(Carol Stream, Illinois)

Jenny Bezingue discovered polymer clay in the early 1990s. Over time, she has incorporated other jewelry-making techniques and media with polymer clay work. She is a founding member of the Chicago Area Polymer Clay Guild and teaches polymer clay, metal clay, and beadwork classes. She serves as the editor of a paper crafting magazine and contributor to other craft magazines. (jennybez@earthlink.net)

Leslie Blackford
(Munfordville, Kentucky)

Leslie Blackford has been working in polymer clay for more than 10 years, and her work has been featured in gallery and museum shows. She has contributed to books on polymer, and taught alongside well-known polymer artists. Her business, Moodywoods, is named after The Moodywoods of Hart County, Kentucky. Nature provides great inspiration for Leslie's fertile imagination, which is expressed through her sculptural creations. (www.scrtc.com/~turtles4/)

Louise Fischer Cozzi
(Brooklyn, New York)

After receiving a BFA at Pratt Institute in graphic design, Louise Fischer Cozzi pursued fiberarts and polymer clay. Since 1991, she has been working in polymer clay. Her love for typography and fiberarts informs her current work. Her work has been featured in magazines such as *Belle Armoire*, *Bead and Button*, and *Lapidary Journal*. She shows and sells her work at galleries and museum shops across the country. She also teaches polymer clay workshops. (www.LouiseFischerCozzi.com)

Jeffrey Lloyd Dever
(Laurel, Maryland)

Jeffrey Lloyd Dever has worked for nearly 30 years in illustration and graphic design. For 20 years, he has been the president of Dever Designs and its Fresh Art Subsidiary. His most recent passion is creating jewelry and vessels made of polymer clay and mixed media. He pioneered polymer clay techniques in form-built hollowware and reinforced armatures. Each piece is an original sculptural exercise, and nature informs his aesthetic. (jeff@deverdesigns.com)

Lindly Haunani
(Cabin John, Maryland)

Lindly Haunani holds a BFA in Printmaking from Carnegie-Mellon University. Since 1989, her polymer clay work has appeared in more than 60 juried and invitational shows in both galleries and museums. Her work has been published in several books and magazines. She is a founding member of the National Polymer Clay Guild and the editor for the POLYinforMER, the Guild's newsletter. She is known for her teaching and work in the area of color blending. (www.lindlyhaunani.com)

Jacqueline Lee
(Springville, Utah)

Jacqueline Lee is a well-known polymer clay artist, author, and instructor. She also does project design and consulting work for several major publishers. Her work has been featured in more than 20 books, and she has published two children's craft books. (www.jacquelineleeonline.com)

Wendy Wallin Malinow
(Portland, Oregon)

Wendy Wallin Malinow is an artist and freelance illustrator. She began working with polymer clay in the late 1980s and, since then, has won numerous awards for her work. Currently she is using polymer in various mixed media combinations. She has illustrated 15 books and consulted on several craft books.

Sandra McCaw
(Alstead, New Hampshire)

Sandra McCaw studied illustration at the Boston Museum School and The School of the Worcester Art Museum. She worked as an illustrator and graphic designer for several years. Her polymer clay work has been shown in exhibitions at locations such as Bryn Mawr College in Philadelphia, Galeria Mesa in Arizona, and Arrowmont School of Crafts in Tennessee. Her work has been featured in five books, and she has published videos on her canework known as "The McCaw Method." (sandramccaw@hotmail.com)

Mari O'Dell
(Annapolis, Maryland)

Mari O'Dell was born and raised in the New York City area. She trained as a potter with a particular interest in ceramic tiles. She was a public school teacher in suburban Washington, DC, for 32 years. She used polymer clay to teach color mixing and jewelry techniques to her students. Since she began working in this medium, she has taught a variety of workshops and classes. She has participated in invitational shows at Baltimore Clay Works and written several articles for *Bead and Button* magazine. She has also produced two instructional videotapes on techniques for Polymer Clay Express.

Pier & Penina
(Mill Valley, California)

Alexis Pier and Penina Meisels are San Francisco Bay Area artisans who create contemporary art jewelry. Alexis Pier earned a BFA from The School of Visual Arts in Manhattan. Her professional careers included positions in medical photography and hi-tech marketing. In 2001, Alexis' creative drive was re-channeled to the medium of polymer clay. Penina Meisels attended The School of Visual Arts in Manhattan and earned a BA from The New School for Social Research in Manhattan. She turned her creative energies to the camera and for over 23 years achieved success as a nationally known advertising photographer before working in polymer clay. (www.pierandpenina.com)

Stephanie Jones Rubiano
(Rancho Viejo, Texas)

Stephanie Jones Rubiano studied marine biology in college, and then worked in Houston as a technician in the environmental and quality control testing departments of an oil company. During her time in Houston, she discovered rubberstamping and paper crafting, which led to her exploration of other media such as bookbinding and polymer clay. Her polymer clay beads using the mokume gane technique were the subject for her first article in a 2002 issue of *Belle Armoire*. Her work has been published in several other magazines and books.

SL Savarick
(Los Angeles, California)

Before SL Savarick found polymer clay, he worked as a professional dancer, pastry chef, bodybuilder, and graphic artist. Today, he works in his Los Angeles studio creating polymer clay inro, minaudiere, art purses, and jewelry. He has taught art and design courses at Parsons School of Design, The Corcoran School of Art, and The Maryland Institute College of Art. He teaches polymer clay, screenprinting, digital art, and design techniques across the country. (www.slsavarickstudio.com)

Judith Skinner
(Prescott, Arizona)

Judith Skinner discovered her inner artist in 1985 but was told to learn to draw before she could use it! "Fortunately," she says, "I discovered polymer clay in 1995 and forgot all about drawing..." In 1996, she developed the well-known polymer technique now known as the Skinner Blend. She says about her current life: "I'm living my dream in a cabin in a small mountain town. I live with two dogs, a varying number of puppies, two cats, and polymer clay everywhere! My work is in two local cooperative galleries. I lead workshops locally and with guilds around the country. What more could I want?" (www.judithskinner.com)

Julia Converse Sober
(DeKalb, Illinois)

Julia Converse Sober's interest in the sciences led her to her current career in radiation protection at Northern Illinois University. She discovered polymer clay in 1991 and found it to be the perfect portable art material for a career involving lots of travel. A few years later Julia's career and her interest in art intersected when she enrolled as a BFA candidate in Northern Illinois' Metals program. In her spare time Julia teaches workshops in design, jewelry construction, and various polymer clay techniques. Her work has been published in several Lark books including *400 Polymer Clay Designs*. (www.juliasober.com).

METRIC CONVERSIONS

INCHES	CENTIMETERS
$1/8$	3 mm
$1/4$	6 mm
$3/8$	9 mm
$1/2$	1.3
$5/8$	1.6
$3/4$	1.9
$7/8$	2.2
1	2.5
$1 1/4$	3.1
$1 1/2$	3.8
$1 3/4$	4.4
2	5
$2 1/2$	6.25
3	7.5
$3 1/2$	8.8
4	10
$4 1/2$	11.3
5	12.5
$5 1/2$	13.8
6	15
7	17.5
8	20
9	22.5
10	25
11	27.5
12	30
1 ft	30
2 ft	60
3 ft	120
4 ft	150
5 ft	180
6 ft	210
7 ft	240
8 ft	270
9 ft	300
10 ft	330

INDEX